Published by City Christian Publishing
9200 NE Fremont
Portland, Oregon 97220

Printed in U.S.A.

> City Christian Publishing is a ministry of City Bible Church and is dedicated to serving the local church and its leaders through the production and distribution of quality restoration materials.
>
> It is our prayer that these materials, proven in the context of the local church, will equip leaders in exalting the Lord and extending His kingdom.
>
> *For a free catalog of additional resources from City Christian Publishing please call 1-800-777-6057 or visit our web site at www.citychristianpublishing.com.*

Empowering Your Preaching – Student Handbook
© Copyright 2002 by City Christian Publishing
All Rights Reserved

ISBN 1-886849-91-9

No portion of this book may be reproduced, stored in a retrieval system, or transmitted in any form or by any means electronic, mechanical photocopy, recording, or any other except for brief quotations in printed reviews, without the prior permission of the Publisher. Rights for publishing this book in other languages are contracted by City Christian Publishing.

Empowering Your Preaching

Section 1: Seminar Notes
1. Preaching and Preachers 1
2. Identifying Levels of Word Ministry 6
3. Twenty-one Signs of Shallow Preaching 8
4. The Preacher and the Word of God 11
5. The Preacher as the Feeder of the Flock 17
6. The 32 Proven Laws for the Preacher 25
7. The Preacher's God-Thought to God-Message 31
8. Endnotes 37

Section 2: Resource Material
1. Gaining a Biblical Perspective on Preaching 38
2. History of Preaching 42
3. Teaching the Church How to Listen 43
4. Simple Steps in Evaluating Your Preaching 45
5. Voice Dynamics 47
6. The Pentecostal Approach to Scripture 49
7. So What's Cooking 51
8. A Preacher's Basic Research Library 52
9. Limited Bibliography on Preaching 53

Section 3: Sermons 54
1. Believer and Spiritual Warfare 55
2. Building Gate Churches for the 21st Century 60
3. Call to Be Equipped 67
4. Call to Cell Commitment 74
5. Kingdom Priorities: Jesus' Laws of Living 79
6. Kingdom Priorities: Renewing Kingdom Lifestyle 83
7. Preparation and Hindrances to Prayer 88
8. Responding to the Call to Become a Church of Intercession 93
9. Rewards of a Renewed Soul 97
10. The Unsearchable Riches of Christ's Mercy 100
11. We Can Touch the World 104
12. Weaving through Building Relationships 109

Empowering Your Preaching

Preaching and Preachers

Preaching Scriptures

Isaiah 61:1 The Spirit of the Lord God is upon Me, because the Lord has anointed Me to *preach* good tidings to the poor; He has sent Me to heal the brokenhearted, to proclaim liberty to the captives, and the opening of the prison to those who are bound.

Amos 8:11 "Behold, the days are coming," says the Lord God, "That I will send a famine on the land, not a famine of bread, nor a thirst for water, but of *hearing the words of the Lord*."

I Timothy 2:7 For which I was appointed a *preacher* and an apostle—I am speaking the truth in Christ and not lying—a teacher of the Gentiles in faith and truth.

I Timothy 4:13 Till I come, give attention to reading, to *exhortation*, to doctrine.

Charles Spurgeon

II Timothy 4:2 *Preach* the word! Be ready in season and out of season. Convince, rebuke, exhort, with all longsuffering and teaching.

Titus 2:1 But as for you, *speak the things* which are proper for sound doctrine:

Luke 16:16 The law and the prophets were until John. Since that time the kingdom of God has been *preached*, and everyone is pressing into it.

II Peter 2:5 And did not spare the ancient world, but saved Noah, one of eight people, a *preacher* of righteousness, bringing in the flood on the world of the ungodly;

Matthew 3:1 In those days John the Baptist came *preaching* in the wilderness of Judea,

Matthew 4:17 From that time Jesus began to *preach* and to say, "Repent, for the kingdom of heaven is at hand."

Matthew 10:7 And as you go *preach*, saying, The kingdom of heaven is at hand.

Matthew 24:14 And this gospel of the kingdom will be *preached* in all the world as a witness to all the nations, and then the end will come.

Jonathan Edwards

Titus 1:3 But has in due time manifested His word through *preaching*, which was committed to me according to the commandment of God our Savior;

Colossians 1:28 Him we *preach*, warning every man and teaching every man in all wisdom, that we may present every man perfect in Christ Jesus.

Haggai 1:13 Then Haggai, the Lord's messenger, *spoke the Lord's message* to the people, saying, "I am with you, says the Lord."

Empowering Your Preaching

Acts 6:4	But we will give ourselves continually to prayer and to the *ministry of the word*.
Mark 16:15	And He said to them, Go into all the world and *preach* the gospel to every creature.
I Corinthians 9:16	For if I *preach* the gospel, I have nothing to boast of, for necessity is laid upon me; yes, woe is me if I do not *preach* the gospel!
II Corinthians 4:5	For we do not *preach* ourselves, but Christ Jesus the Lord, and ourselves your bondservants for Jesus' sake.
II Timothy 2:15	Be diligent to present yourself approved to God, a worker who does not need to be ashamed, *rightly dividing* the word of truth.
II Timothy 3:16	All Scripture is given by inspiration of God, and is profitable for *doctrine*, for reproof, for correction, for instruction in righteousness,
Romans 10:14	How then shall they call on Him in whom they have not believed? And how shall they believe in Him of whom they have not heard? And how shall they hear without a *preacher*?

Preaching

1. **Hebrew definition of the word "preach":** An annunciation of a specific message with specific recipients, with an intent to elicit a specific response, a planned encounter, a confrontation.

2. **Greek definition of the word "preach":** "To publicly proclaim or announce news of something to come. It speaks of a forerunner who delivers a message with authority."

John Calvin

3. **Webster's Dictionary:** To exhort in a tedious and tiresome manner.

4. **Philip Brooks**: "Preaching is truth mediated through personality. All of one's faculties are engaged."

5. **Martin Lloyd Jones:** "Preaching is something very difficult to define. It is certainly not a matter of rules or regulations. Preaching is something that one recognizes when one hears it. True preaching is God acting. It is not just a man uttering words; it is God using him."

6. **Jay E. Adams:** "Preaching must include the presence of the Holy Spirit, apart from whom preaching is worthless, indeed, injurious. So then preaching necessarily involves content in the form of a biblical message, a preacher, an occasion, listeners, and the Holy Spirit.

7. **John MacArthur:** "Preaching requires that an expositor be one who explains scripture by laying open the text to public view in order to set forth its meaning, explain what is difficult to understand and make appropriate application… Preaching is logical in flow, doctrinal in content, pastoral in concern, imaginative in pattern, relevant in application."

8. **Warren Wiersbe:** "Preaching is the communicating of God's truth by God's servant to meet the needs of people."

Empowering Your Preaching

9. **Herbert W. Cragg:** "To me four words are involved in preparation and preaching of the word: exegesis, exposition, illustration and application."

10. **Bernard Manning:** "Preaching is the manifestation of the incarnate word from the written word by the spoken word."

11. **Merril F. Unger:** "True preaching is emphatically not preaching about the Bible but preaching the Bible. It begins in the Bible and ends in the Bible and all that intervenes springs from the Bible. It is preaching that is Bible-centered."

12. **F.B. Meyer:** "There are five considerations that must be met in every successful sermon. There should be an appeal to the reason, to the conscience, to the imagination, to the emotions, and to the will, and for each of these there is no method so serviceable as systematic exposition."

Preachers

1. **Henry Ward Beecher:** "His sermons were not well organized or profound, but were kindling, suggestive and moving with great imagination and eloquent."

2. **Philip Brooks:** "He preached from manuscripts. His messages had beauty, vigor, and a sweeping flow that held his hearers spellbound. He was a great thinker and usually dealt with one major idea, turning it around and round to point outs its facets."

3. **G. Campbell Morgan:** "Achieved the highest standards of perfection as an expository preacher."

George Campbell Morgan

4. **Charles Spurgeon:** Spurgeon possessed natural gifts: a magnificent bell voice, a rare and ready command of homespun English, a racy style of speaking, a saving sense of humor, deep insight into the spiritual needs of the common man, and an utter devotion to Christ. He took no more than one page of notes into the pulpit and spoke 140 words per minute for 40 minutes.

5. **George Whitefield**: "Endowed with a marvelous preaching voice, he has been called the prince of the pulpit. He preached with boldness, directness, eloquence, deep feeling and perfect gestures. His vivid imagination and sonorous voice charmed the multitudes."

6. **Jonathan Edwards:** "His sermons were long, heavy and contained many divisions."

7. **Robert Murray McCheyne:** "When he appeared in the pulpit, even before he had uttered a single word, people would begin to weep silently. The very sight of the man gave the impression that he had come from the presence of God and that he was to deliver a message from God."

Robert McCheyne

8. **Richard Cecil:** "To love to preach is one thing. To love those to whom we preach quite another."

9. **Samuel Rutherford:** "I preached as never sure to preach again, and as a dying man to dying men."

Empowering Your Preaching

10. **Bishop William A. Quale:** "Preaching is the art of making a sermon and delivering it? Why no, that's not preaching! Preaching is the art of making a preacher and delivering that; preaching is the outrush of the soul in speech."

11. **Puritans:** "True preaching is the most exciting labor in the world, and a man can make nothing of it unless he puts everything into it."

12. **Joseph Parker:** "The preacher is not an author reading his own manuscript. He is a voice, a fire, a herald, bold and eager in his sacred work, an orator speaking in heaven's name and strength."

13. **John Henry Newman:** "He laid his finger, how gently yet how powerfully, on some inner place in the hearer's heart and told him things about himself he had never known until then."

John Henry Newman

14. **John Calvin:** "Calvin understood preaching to be the explication of scripture. The words of scripture are the source and content of preaching. As an expositor, Calvin brought to the task of preaching all the skills of a humanist scholar. As an interpreter, Calvin explicated the text, seeking its natural, its true, its scriptural meaning, also its application word by word. So he applied scripture sentence by sentence to the life and experience of the congregation."

15. **John Stott:** "The systematic preaching of the word is impossible without the systematic studying of it. We must daily soak ourselves in the scriptures."

16. **Martin Luther:** "Prayer, meditation and suffering makes a preacher. The stars shine the brightest when the night is the darkest and God is able to give us songs in the night."

17. **John Wesley**: He told preachers they should invite, convince, offer Christ and build up the saints. Every sermon should have each of those elements in some measure. He wrote 231 books, preached 40,000 sermons and traveled by horse over 250,000 miles.

18. **F.B. Meyer:** Throughout his life he made this commend about himself, "I am only an ordinary man. I have no special gifts. I am no orator, no scholar, no profound thinker. If I have done anything for Christ and my generation, it is because I have given myself entirely to Christ and then tried to do whatever He wanted me to do." Charles Spurgeon said of F.B. Meyer as a preacher, "Meyer preaches as a man who has seen God face to face."

John Wesley

19. **Origen** (AD 180-253): "I do not disdain rhetoric itself, but rather the misuse of it. Regarding style, but a lucid discourse, the splendor of eloquence and the art of arguing with propriety are admitted to the service of the word of God."

20. **Archbishop Leighton:** People criticized Leighton because he did not preach to the times. His replay was, "While so many are preaching to the times, may not one poor brother preach for eternity?"

Empowering Your Preaching

21. **D.L. Moody:** Those who have analyzed his preaching tell us that his sermons averaged about half an hour in length. He used short sentences, averaging about 17 words, and short words, 80% of them monosyllables. He used few adjectives and adverbs, but majored on verbs with a lot of action. He used the language of the marketplace and sought to reach the common man. "We have too many orators. I am tired and sick of these silver-tongued orators."

22. **Jay Adams:** "The preacher is there to deliver the message of God, a message from God to the people, a mouthpiece of God. He is there to do something to the people, produce results, influence people. It should change the person listening in every way—emotionally, mentally, directionally, spiritually."

23. **George A. Buttrick:** "Preaching is, in one regard, like bringing up children. We know all about it until we have to do it, then we know nothing."

John Wesley arose at four o'clock in the morning, and preached at least twice each day, often three or four times. It has been estimated that he traveled forty-five hundred miles annually, mostly upon horseback."

Empowering Your Preaching

Identifying Levels of Word Ministry
I Timothy 3:1,17; II Timothy 2:9; 2:15; 4:2

I. **LEVELS OF WORD MINISTRY**

   A. Depends on the Calling

      1. Saint

      2. Deacon

      3. Elder

      4. Five-Fold Ministry

   B. Depends on the Gifting and Ability

      1. Gift of preaching or teaching

      2. Ability and capacity

      3. Desire and commitment to excellence

> "A natural faculty in the preacher should be a capacity for hard work. No man who is not prepared to work himself to death has any right in the ministry at all."
> (Ian MacPherson)

II. **LEVELS OF DISCIPLINE AND DESIRE**

   A. The Devotional Reader and Casual Researcher

   B. The Serious Reader and Dedicated Researcher

   C. The Systematic Reader and Serious Researcher

   D. The Skilled Reader and Serious Preacher

III. **THE PREACHER DETERMINES HIS/HER LEVEL**

   A. The Preacher Himself or Herself
      (Rom 12:7-8; I Corinthians 12:28-29; Eph 4:11-12)

      1. The Preacher's Calling

      2. The Preacher's Dedication

Susanna Wesley

Empowering Your Preaching

      3.   The Preacher's Education

      4.   The Preacher's Exposure

      5.   The Preacher's Experience

B.   The Preacher's Dedication to the Basics

      1.   Theology, Apologetics, Bible Knowledge and Church History

      2.   Hermeneutics (Luke 24:25-35)
           a.   The Context Principle
           b.   The First Mention Principle
           c.   The Comparative Principle
           d.   The Progressive Principle
           e.   The Election Principle
           f.   The Covenantal Principle
           g.   The Christo-centric Principle
           h.   The Moral Principle
           i.   The Symbolic Principle
           j.   The Parabolic Principle
           k.   The Allegorical Principle
           l.   The Interpreting of Prophecy
           m.   The Complete Mention Principle
           n.   The Breach Principle
           o.   The Typical Principle

      3.   Homiletical Skills: The field of sermon preparation and delivery

      4.   Communication Skills

      5.   Understanding the Present Culture

      6.   Research Methods and Skills
           a.   Word Studies
           b.   Character Studies
           c.   Place Studies
           d.   Passage Studies
           e.   Book Studies
           f.   Expositional Studies (verse by verse, passage)
           g.   Topical Studies
           h.   Typical Studies

      7.   Research Tools

> John Wesley would not suffer any man to minister in his societies unless he undertook to devote a minimum of five hours in every twenty-four to diligent delving into the word of God.

> "Time in the word need not exceed two hours, should not be less than one hour each morning. The preacher must be consistent, not careless." (Watchman Nee)

Empowering Your Preaching

21 Signs of Shallow Preaching
I Timothy 4:16

INTRODUCTION

A magazine article stated that television is aimed at the twelve-year-old mind and many churches seem to be catering to this same goal. Preachers seem to be more story-minded with few scriptures than they are word-minded. Shallow preaching appears to be the modern way of the American pulpit. Shallow preachers produce shallow Christians, which produces a shallow church. Charles Bridges offers some thought along the line of shallow preaching: "With some, confidence supplies the place of premeditation, a Bible and concordance, with a few sermon notes, or even the gift of tolerable fluency. These are not sufficient material to stand up in the name of the great God, but what is solid is alone permanent!" (Proverbs 27:7-8; Psalm 130:1; Proverbs 3:20; Mark 4:5)

I. DEFINING SHALLOW PREACHING

A. Definition: Not deep, having little depth, superficial, empty, weak, thin

B. Synonym: Empty-headed, feather-brained, flimsy, frivolous, trivial, petty, sketchy, wishy-washy.

C. Conceptual: To be shallow-hearted, having no depth of feeling, to be without depth of thought or judgement.

D. The Laver Principle (Exodus 30:18-28; 31:9; 40:7,11,30; James 1:25-27; 2:12)

> "Often, I'm afraid, the church is a place where preachers preach, not out of their depths, but out of their shallows." (Fredrick Buechner)

II. DESCRIBING SHALLOW PREACHERS

A. **Professional Preachers**: Masters of language who are skilled in the art of preaching. They view this as a great career choice and impress people but to not move people spiritually.

B. **Pretending Preachers**: Orators with no calling or anointing to do what they are doing, they walk, talk and dress like a preacher but it is only a pretense.

C. **Pulpiteer Preachers**: Showmen who play the crowd, they know the techniques and learn the psychology of crowd control.

D. **Entertaining Preachers**: The form becomes more important than the substance; eloquence, humor, oratory.

E. **Psychology Preachers**: They start with the problem and work toward an answer, not necessarily ending with the Bible.

F. **Persuasion Preachers**: Using a debate-type delivery and an academic approach, they are more interested in being right than in reaching people.

Empowering Your Preaching

G. **"Fit into the service" Preachers**: Worship and other things take precedence and it takes so much time to produce the atmosphere that there is no time to preach in the atmosphere.

H. **Talking Preachers**: Preaching without unction and without heart, they give a "talk" or a "lecture".

> A Methodist bishop once said of a preacher in his district, "He is supernaturally dull. No one could be that dull without divine aid."

III. **21 SIGNS OF SHALLOW PREACHING**
(John 1:23; Acts 29:19,31; II Corinthians 2:4; II Timothy 3:16; 4:2-3)

A. Shallow preaching is superficial preaching

B. Shallow preaching is "without depth of feeling" preaching

C. Shallow preaching is "without depth of thought" preaching

D. Shallow preaching is empty preaching

E. Shallow preaching is flat preaching

F. Shallow preaching is hollow preaching

G. Shallow preaching is half-baked preaching

H. Shallow preaching is light-weight preaching

I. Shallow preaching is meaningless preaching

J. Shallow preaching is showy preaching

K. Shallow preaching is "adding to" preaching

L. Shallow preaching is myopic (short-sighted) preaching

M. Shallow preaching is skimpy "cutting the corners" preaching

N. Shallow preaching is stereotyped, average and ordinary preaching

> "There are only three kinds of sermons. Those that are dull, those that are duller and those that are inconceivably dull." (William MacGregor)

Empowering Your Preaching

    O.   Shallow preaching is substitute, artificial preaching

    P.   Shallow preaching is tasteless preaching

    Q.   Shallow preaching is unfaithful (cheating) preaching

    R.   Shallow preaching is unintentional preaching

    S.   Shallow preaching is reckless preaching

    T.   Shallow preaching is routine, professionalism preaching

    U.   Shallow preaching is mean preaching

IV. THE REMEDY FOR SHALLOW PREACHING

    A.   A fresh time in the word, alone and away, with fasting and prayer

    B.   A fresh commitment to word-preaching as a messenger of God

    C.   A new fresh relationship to the Holy Spirit

    D.   An open, honest exposing and evaluating of your ministry

    E.   A possible change of preaching method and the purpose of your preaching

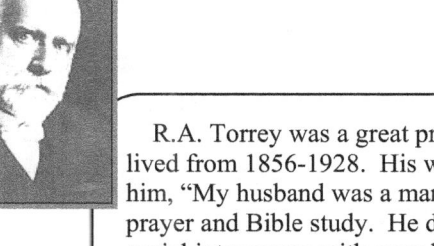

R.A. Torrey was a great preacher who lived from 1856-1928. His wife said of him, "My husband was a man of much prayer and Bible study. He denied himself social intercourse with even his best friends in order that he might have time for prayer, study and the preparation for his work."

Empowering Your Preaching

The Preacher and the Word of God
II Timothy 4:2; Amos 8:11

"Thou art a preacher of the word; Mind thy business.
(Old Puritan saying)

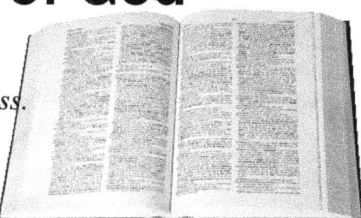

INTRODUCTION
The preacher is called to preach the Word of God accurately and faithfully. There are many temptations to preach other things and end up neglecting the primacy of preaching the powerful, living word of God. Preaching the word can be unpopular in an entertainment-oriented, short attention span generation, but preaching the word is a must if we are to fulfill our calling. The greatest power ever known is the spoken word of God. It has called worlds into being, toppled empires, healed and comforted the sick, shaken the proud and resurrected the dead. Yet in far too many pulpits, that powerful word lies unopened, unspoken and therefore uncomprehended. (Acts 2:41; 4:29,31; I:4; 10:36-37,44; 11:1,19; 12:24; 13:48-49; 19:20; Psalm 138:2-3; Isaiah 55:11; Jeremiah 1:12)

Anglican Confession: The scripture of God is the heavenly meat of our souls. It is a light lantern to our feet. It is a sure, steadfast and everlasting instrument of salvation. It comforteth, maketh glad, cheereth, and cherisheth our conscience. The words of Holy Scripture be called, words of everlasting life, for they be God's instrument, ordained for the same purpose. They have power to turn, though God's promise and being received in a faithful heart, they have ever a heavenly spiritual working in them.

John Wesley: "I am a creature of a day, passing through life as an arrow through the air. I am a spirit, coming from God, and returning to God; just hovering over the great gulf; a few months hence I am no more seen; I drop into an unchangeable eternity! I want to know one thing – the way to heaven... God himself has condescended to teach the way. He hath written it down in a book. O give me that Book! At any price, give me the book of God!"[1]

I. **THE POWERFUL WORKING OF THE WORD OF GOD**
   Hebrews 4:12
   NKJ: For the word of God is living and powerful, and sharper than any two-edged sword, piercing even to the division of soul and spirit, and of joints and marrow, and is a discerner of the thoughts and intents of the heart.
   Amplified: For the Word that God speaks is alive and full of power [making it active, operative, energizing, and effective]; it is sharper than any two-edged sword, penetrating to the dividing line of the breath of life (soul) and [the immortal] spirit, and of joints and marrow [of the deepest parts of our nature], exposing and sifting and analyzing and judging the very thoughts and purposes of the heart.
   The Message: His powerful word is sharp as a surgeon's scalpel, cutting through everything, whether doubt or defense, laying us open to listen and obey. Nothing and no one is impervious to God's word. We can't get away from it—no matter what.

Empowering Your Preaching

A. **The Word of God**
This is the spoken and written word of God and cannot be taken lightly. (John 10:35; Luke 16:17; II Timothy 3:16; Romans 3:2; Acts 7:38)

B. **The Word is Living**
(John 6:33; I Peter 1:23; Acts 7:38)
"God's Message is a living and active power (TCNT), the Divine Reason (Wade) is alive and full of power in action (Williams), lives and is active (Becky) and workable (Klingensmith) and energetic (Wilson)." [1]

C. **The Word is Active, Energetic, Powerful**
(John 1:12; Philippians 3:21; Colossians 1:29; I Corinthians 1:18)
"God's Message is a living and active power (TCNT), the Divine Reason (Wade) is alive and full of power in action (Williams), lives and is active (Becky) and workable (Klingensmith) and energetic (Wilson)." [2]

> "The Bible is alive, it speaks to me; it has feet, it runs after me; it has hands, it lays hold on me." (Martin Luther)

D. **The Word is Sharper**
(Eph 6:17; Rev 1:16; Isaiah 49:2)
Keener than any two-edged blade (Wade) and more cutting than any two-edged sword (Wilson), any double-edged sword (Williams), a sword that cuts both ways (NLT). [3]

E. **The Word is Piercing, Penetrating, Dividing**
(I Thess 5:23; I Corinth 15:45)
It can slice between (SEB). It is a judge of (Klingensmith), penetrating deeply enough to split soul and spirit (Adams) cutting through even to a separation of life and breath (Wilson), even to the severance of soul from spirit (Montgomery). [4]

F. **The Word Judges the Thoughts and Intentions of the Heart**
(Psalm 139:1-3,12; John 12:47-48)
"It is keen in judging the thoughts (Norlie). It can tell the difference between the desires and the intentions of the human mind (SEB) and detecting the inmost thoughts (TCNT) and is a sifter and analyzer of the reflections and conceptions of the heart (Wuest). It is a judge of the sentiments and thoughts of the heart (Concordant), the very thoughts (Montgomery).

Empowering Your Preaching

II. **THE POWERFUL EFFECTS OF THE WORD OF GOD**

   A. The Balanced Ministry of Jesus and the Early Church (Matthew 4:23; 9:35)

   1. The Three-Fold Cord of Jesus' Ministry
       Stretching from the inception of the Christian faith down to this very hour, there is an unbroken succession of preachers and teachers. Wherever preaching was at its best, the sermons (as exemplified in the sermons of Peter, Stephen, and Paul) contain a large element of word content.
       a. Teaching: systematic instruction (used 217 times)
       b. Preaching: anointed proclamation (used 140 times)
       c. Healing: supernatural works of the Holy Spirit.

   2. Jesus: The Teacher and The Preacher
       Jesus was frequently called "Rabbi" or "Teacher." Of the ninety times the Lord was addressed, as recorded in the gospels, sixty times he was called "Rabbi". Furthermore, the thought of the speaker in at least part of the thirty remaining cases was directed toward Jesus as a teacher, for the Greek word *aidaskalos*, which refers to "one who teaches concerning the things of God and the duties of man," is translated sometimes "teacher" and sometimes "master." (John 3:2; Luke 18:18; Luke 10:25; Mark 9:38; Matt 22:16; 7:28-29; 28:19-20; Luke 19:39; 20:39; Mark 6:6; Eph 4:11)

   3. The First Church Emphasized Continual Teaching and Preaching (Acts 5:42; 6:7; 11:26; 15:35; 20:20; 28:31; 13:1; I Corinthians 12:28)

   B. Biblical Words Used to Describe the Teaching and Preaching Process

   1. Old Testament Terms

       a. **Discipline** (*lamadh*): to beat
          A very common word for "to teach", it may have meant "to beat with a rod, to chastise and may have originally referred to the striking and goading of beasts by which they were curbed and trained. By a noble evolution the term came to describe the process of disciplining and training men in war, religion and life (Is 2:3; Hos 10:11; Micah 4:2). As teaching is both a condition and an accompaniment of disciplining, the word often means simply "to teach or to inform" (II Chronicles 17:7; Psalm 71:17; Proverbs 5:13). The glory of teaching was its harmony with the will of God, its source in God's authority and its purpose to secure spiritual obedience (Deuteronomy 4:5,14; 31:12-13).

Empowering Your Preaching

b. **Law** (*yarah*): to cast
The teaching idea from which the law was derived is expressed by a very which means to throw, to cast as an arrow or lot. It is also used of thrusting the hand forth to point out or show clearly (Gen 46:28; Ex 15:25). The original ideas is easily changed into an educational concept since the teacher puts forth new ideas and facts as a sower casts seed into the ground. But the process of teaching was not considered external and mechanical but internal and vital (Ex 35:34-35; II Chron 6:27).

c. **Discernment** (*bin*): to separate
To cause to distinguish or separate. The word meaning "to separate or to distinguish" is often used in a causative sense to signify "to teach". The idea of teaching was not an aggregation of facts bodily transferred like merchandise. Real learning followed genuine teaching. This word suggests a sound psychological basis for a good pedagogy. The function of teaching might be exercised with reference to the solution of difficult problems, the interpretation of God's will or the manner of a godly life (Daniel 8:16,26; Nehemiah 8:7-9; Psalm 119:34).

d. **Wisdom** (*sakhal*): to be wise
The verb from which the various nominal forms for "wisdom" are derived means "to look at, to behold, to view" and in the causative stem describes the process by which one is enabled to see for himself what had never before entered his physical or intellectual field of consciousness. The noun indicates a wise person or sage whose mission is to instruct others in the ways of the Lord (Proverbs 16:23; 21:11). In Daniel 12:3 we read "They that are wise (teachers) shall shine as the brightness of the firmament."

e. **Knowledge** (*yadha*): to see
This verb literally means to see and consequently to perceive, to know, to come to know and cause to know or teach. It describes the act of knowing as both progressive and completed. The causative conception signifies achievement in the sphere of instruction. It is used of the interpretation and application by Moses of the principles of the law of God (Exodus 18:16,20), of the elucidation of life's problems by the sages (Pr 9:9; 22:19) and of constant providential guidance in the way of life (Ps 16:11).

f. **Illumination** (*zahar*): to shine
This verbal root signifies "to shine, to bring to light" and when applied to the intellectual sphere indicates the function of teaching to be one of illumination. Ignorance is darkness, knowledge is light. Moses was to teach the people statutes and laws or to enlighten them on the principles and precepts of God's revelation (Ex 18:20). The service rendered by the teachers –priests, Levites and fathers– sent forth by Jehoshaphat, was one of illumination in the twofold sense of instruction and admonition (II Chr 19:8-10).

John Wesley

g. **Vision** (*ra'-ah*): to see
The literal meaning of this very is "to see" and the nominal form is the ancient name for prophet or authoritative teacher who was expected to have a clear vision of spiritual realities, the will of God, the need of man and the way of life (I Sam 9:9; I Chr 9:22; 2 Chr 16:7).

h. **Inspiration** (*nabha*): to boil up
The most significant word for "prophet" is derived from the verb which means "to boil up or forth like a fountain" and consequently to pour forth words under the impelling power of the spirit of God. The Hebrews used the passive forms of the verb because they considered the thoughts and words of the prophets due not to personal ability but to divine influence. The utterances of the prophets were characterized by instruction, admonition, persuasion and prediction (Deut 18:15-22; Ezek 33:1-20).

i. **Nourishment** (*ra`ah*): to feed a flock
The name "shepherd", so precious in both the Old and New Testaments, comes from a verb meaning "to feed" hence to protect and care for out of a sense of devotion, ownership and responsibility. It is employed with reference to civil rulers in their positions of trust (II Sam 5:2; Jer 23:2), with reference to teachers of virtue and wisdom (Pr 10:21; Eccl 12;11), and preeminently with reference to God as the great Shepherd of His chosen people (Ps 23;1; Hos 4:16). Ezekiel 34 presents an arraignment of the unfaithful shepherds or civil rulers. Psalm 23 reveals Yahweh as the Shepherd of true believers and John 10 shows how religious teachers are shepherds under Jesus the Good Shepherd.

2. New Testament Terms

   a. **Instruction** (*didasko*): to teach
   The usual word for "teach" in the New Testament signifies either to hold a discourse with others in order to instruct them or to deliver a didactic discourse where there may not be direct personal and verbal participation. In the former sense it describes the interlocutory method, the interplay of the ideas and words between pupils and teachers, and in the latter use it refers to the more formal monologues designed especially to give information (Matthew 4:23; 13:36; John 6:59; I Cor 4:17; I Tim 2:12). A teacher is one who performs the function or fills the office of instruction. Ability and fitness for the work are required (Rom 2:20; Heb 5:12). The title refers to Jewish teachers (John 1:38), to John the Baptist (Lk 3:12), to Jesus (Jn 3:2; 8;4) and to Paul (I Tim 2:7; II Tim 1:11), and to instructors in the early church (Acts 13:1; Rom 12:7; I Cor 12:28). Teaching, like preaching, was an integral part of the work of an apostle (Mt 28:19; Mk 16:15; Eph 4:1).

   b. **Acquisition** (*Manthano*): to learn
   The central thought of teaching is causing one to learn. Teaching and learning are not scholastic but dynamic and imply personal relationship and activity in the acquisition of knowledge (Mt 11:29; 28:19; Acts 14:21). There were three concentric circles of disciples in the time of our Lord: learners, pupils, superficial followers, the multitude, the body of believers who accepted Jesus as their Master, and the twelve disciples whom Jesus also called apostles.

c. **Presentation** (*paratithemi*): to place beside
   The presentative idea involved in the teaching process is intimately associated with the principle of adaptation. When it is stated that Christ put forth parables unto the people, the sacred writer employs the figure of placing alongside of or near one, hence before him in an accessible position. The food or teaching should be sound, or hygienic, and adapted to the capacity and development of the recipient (Mt 13:24; Mk 8:6 ; Acts 16:34; I Cor 10:27; II Tim 4:3; Heb 5:12-14).

d. **Elucidation** (*diermeneuo*) to interpret
   In the walk to Emmaus, Christ explained to the perplexed disciples the Old Testament scripture in reference to Himself. The work of interpreter is to make truth clear an to effect the edification of the hearer (Lk 24:27; I Cor 12;30; 14:5,13,27).

e. **Exposition** (*ektithemi*): to place out
   The verb literally means "to set or place out" and signifies to bring out the latent and secret ideas of a literary passage or a system of thought and life. Thus Peter interpreted his vision, Aquila and Priscilla unfolded truth to Apollos and Paul expounded the gospel in Rome (Acts 11:4; 18:26; 28:23). True teaching is an educational exposition.

C. Biblical Results of Biblical Teaching and Preaching

1. Divine guidance in life (Psalm 119:105,133)

2. Spiritual cleansing from all things that hinder (Psalm 119:9,11)

3. Spiritual health and vitality (Proverbs 4:4,20-22)

4. Security and safety (Psalm 18:30; 19:8)

5. Established in foundational truths (Hebrews 5:12-14; 6:1-3; I Peter 1:12)

6. Equipped for the work of the Lord (Ephesians 4:11-13)

7. Darkness driven out (I Peter 2:9; I John 1:6-7; Colossians 2:6)

8. Instruction in the principles of warfare (Psalm 18:34; 144:1; II Samuel 22:35)

Empowering Your Preaching

The Preacher as the Feeder of the Flock
Psalm 78:72

INTRODUCTION:
A well-prepared feeder is the prerequisite of a well-fed flock. Many pastors, teachers and other five-fold ministries are finding themselves in a time of pressure and frustration in the area of feeding. Some shepherds are discouraged because of their lack of training, others by their lack of time. In this session we will concentrate on the feeder. The food provided in the word of God never changes: it is pure, powerful and always up-to-date with the needs of the people. This is not always the case with the feeder. He does change and he does not always meet the needs of the people. The reason why the Puritans made such an impact in their time and continue to influence our day with their writings is that they majored on the life-giving power of the Holy Scripture. The Puritan insisted that the preacher's task is to feed their congregations with the contents of the Bible, not the dry husks of their own fancy, but the life-giving words of God.

I. **THE BALANCED MINISTRY OF THE PREACHER (John 21:15-17)**

   A. The Balance of Bosko and Poimano

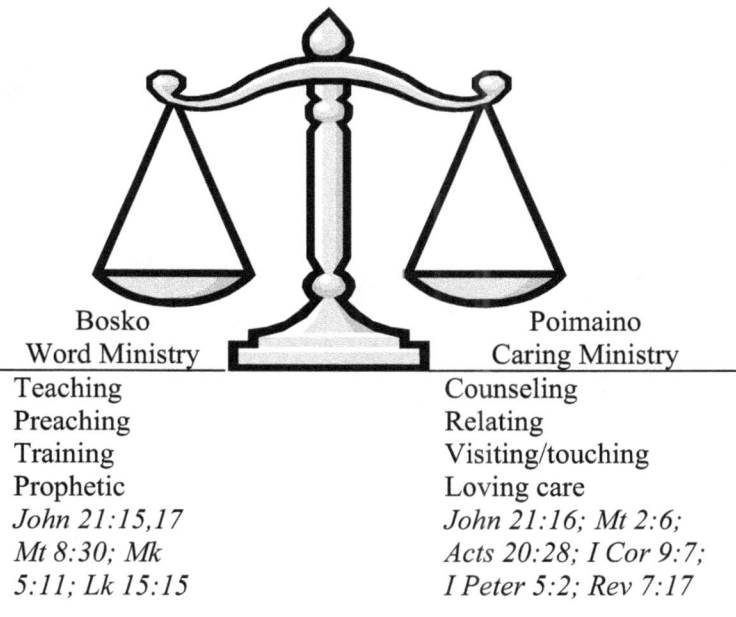

Bosko Word Ministry	Poimaino Caring Ministry
Teaching	Counseling
Preaching	Relating
Training	Visiting/touching
Prophetic	Loving care
John 21:15,17	*John 21:16; Mt 2:6;*
Mt 8:30; Mk	*Acts 20:28; I Cor 9:7;*
5:11; Lk 15:15	*I Peter 5:2; Rev 7:17*

   B. Feeding: The Central Task of The Preacher

   1. Acts 20:28

   2. I Peter 5:2

   3. Jeremiah 3:15

   4. Jeremiah 23:4

Empowering Your Preaching

II. **THE BENCHMARK DECISIONS OF THE PREACHER**
Acts 6:2 Then the twelve summoned the multitude of the disciples and said, "It is not desirable that we should leave the word of God and serve tables."
Amplified: So the Twelve apostles convened the multitude of the disciples and said, It is not seemly or desirable or right that we should have to give up or neglect preaching the word of God in order to attend to serving at tables and superintending the distribution of food.

A. The Common Tables Preachers Are Pressured to Serve

Conflicts, Building Projects, People Expectations, Budgeting Problems, Administration, Busyness, Counseling, Multiple Programs

B. The Two Tables All Preachers Should Serve
Acts 6:4 But we will give ourselves continually to prayer and to the ministry of the word.

1. The Priority of Prayer

    a. H.A. Ironside: "The morning watch is almost as regular as the sunrise." This expositor meditated in his Bible and prayed for an hour and afterward gave himself to more intensive study and further prayer. Rivers of living water overflowed him from his times with God to the crowds that heard him. He insisted, "If we would prevail with men in public, we must prevail with God in secret."

    b. Charles Finney: He lived like Jesus, slipping away to engage in special times of prayer and fasting. Speaking after much prayer, he saw God bring great blessing on his ministry. He was convinced about the importance of prayer. "Without this you are as weak as weakness itself. If you lose your spirit of prayer, you will do nothing or next to nothing although you had the intellectual endowment of an angel. The blessed Lord deliver and preserve his dead church from the guidance and influence of men who know not what it is to pray."

    c. Andrew Blackwood, professor of homiletics at Princeton Theological Seminary, counsels the preacher to lay down one rule and never make an exception. "Start, continue and end with prayer. For in his study the prophet can build his altar and on it lay the wood. There he can lovingly place his sacrificed sermon, but still he knows the fire must come down from God. Come at will, if he prays before he works and if he works in the spirit of prayer."

> "Light praying will make for light preaching. Be up earlier than usual, meditate and pray over it. Steep every sentence of it in the Spirit and pray after it." (Alexander Whyte)

Empowering Your Preaching

2. The Priority of the Word

   a. Deuteronomy 8:3 So He humbled you, allowed you to hunger, and fed you with manna which you did not know nor did your fathers know, that He might make you know that man shall not live by bread alone; but man lives by every word that proceeds from the mouth of the Lord.

   b. Psalm 18:30 As for God, His way is perfect; the word of the Lord is proven; He is a shield to all who trust in Him.

   c. Psalm 119:11 Your word I have hidden in my heart, that I might not sin against You! (See also Psalm 119:16-17,28-29)

   d. Isaiah 55:10-11 For as the rain comes down, and the snow from heaven, and do not return there, but water the earth, and make it bring forth and bud, that it may give seed to the sower and bread to the eater, so shall My word be that goes forth from My mouth; it shall not return to Me void, but it shall accomplish what I please, and it shall prosper in the thing for which I sent it.

   e. Philippians 2:16 Holding fast the word of life, so that I may rejoice in the day of Christ that I have not run in vain or labored in vain.

   f. Colossians 3:16 Let the word of Christ dwell in you richly in all wisdom, teaching and admonishing one another in psalms and hymns and spiritual songs, singing with grace in your hearts to the Lord.

   g. I Thessalonians 2:13 For this reason we also thank God without ceasing, because when you received the word of God which you heard from us, you welcomed it not as the word of men, but as it is in truth, the word of God, which also effectively works in you who believe.

> "To eat into the very soul of the Bible until at last you come to talk scriptural language and your spirit is flavored with the words of the Lord, so that your blood is biblical blood and the very essence of the Bible flows from you." (Charles Spurgeon)

III. THE PREACHER'S COMMON CHALLENGES

   A. The Preacher and the Problem of Spiritual Dullness
      (Ecclesiastes 10:10; Lamentations 4:1; Matthew 15:16; II Corinthians 3:14)

   B. The Preacher and the Principle of Light
      (Job 12:25; 17:12; Psalm 13:3; 36:9; 43:3; 119:130)

   C. The Preacher and the "Message Snatching" Mentality
      (John 5:39; Acts 17:11; Isaiah 38;13; Matthew 22:29)

   D. The Preacher and the "Spermalogos" Temptation
      (Acts 17:18)

E. The Preacher and the Flow of Pure Revelation

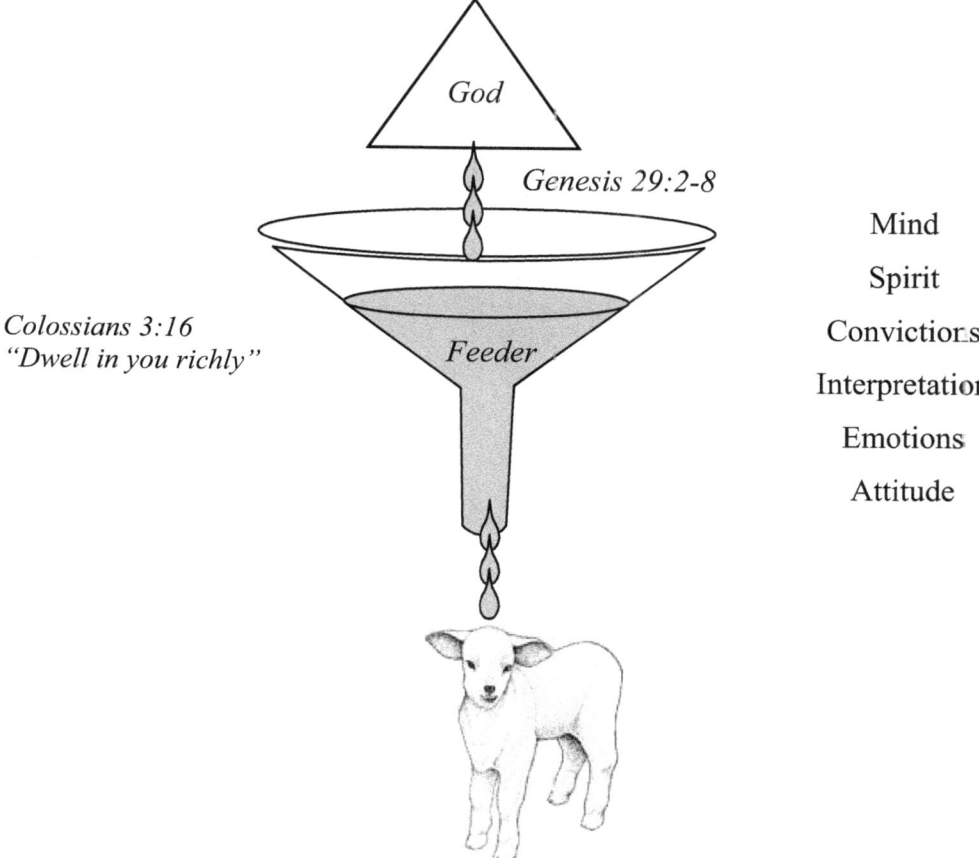

John 7:37; Proverbs 16:22; 18:4; II Peter 2:17

IV. THE PREACHER AND HIS BIBLICAL FUNCTION

A. The preacher as a steward.
(I Corinthians 4:1-2; Isaiah 22:21-22; Mark 14:14; I Timothy 5:14)

B. The preacher as a guardian.
(II Timothy 2:2)

C. The preacher as a herald.
(I Corinthians 1:21,23; II Timothy 2:7; II Timothy 1:11)

D. The preacher as a workman.
(II Timothy 2:15; Revelation 18:22)

Empowering Your Preaching

- E. The preacher as a treasure house.
  (Genesis 43:23; Proverbs 15:6; Isaiah 33:6; Matthew 13:44; II Corinthians 4:7)

- F. The preacher as a sower of seed.
  (Genesis 1:11,29; 47:19; Psalm 126:6; Isaiah 55:10; Matthew 13:34; I Corinthians 3:6; II Corinthians 9:10)

- G. The preacher as a searcher.
  (Proverbs 25:2; Ecclesiastes 3:6; 7:25)

- H. The preacher as a straight cutter.
  (II Timothy 2:15)

> "Preaching exists not for the propagating of views, opinions and ideals but for the proclamation of the mighty acts of God. (James Stewart)

V. **PASTORAL DISCIPLINE IN MAINTAINING A HEALTHY DIET**
(Psalm 23:1-6; Ezekiel 34:10-14,18-19; Zechariah 11:16; John 21:15)

- A. What is a Healthy Diet?
   1. A balanced diet
   2. A consistent diet
   3. A growth-emphasis diet

- B. How to Develop a Healthy Diet?
   1. Evaluate the growth level and maturity of your flock
   2. Evaluate the emphasis in your teaching/preaching over the past year or years.
   3. Determine the specific areas of weakness in the flock (family, prayer, worship, joy, relationships, maturity, giving, vision, etc.)
   4. After evaluation of the flock and your own personal emphasis, you must then determine to meet the needs of the flock through a systematic teaching approach

VI. **METHODS OF FEEDING THE FLOCK**

- A. Book of the Bible: this can be done by chapter or by subject
- B. Chapter of the Bible in a verse by verse expository style
- C. A character of the Bible, revealing principles and insights for daily living

D. Place studies such as Zion, the wilderness, etc.

E. Thematic or subject study through the scriptures to meet a particular need in the flock

F. Methods of preaching usually fall into three types.

1. Topical: Messages usually combine a series of Bible verses that loosely connect with a theme.

2. Textual: Preaching using a short text or passage that generally serves as a gateway into whatever subject the preacher chooses to address.

3. Expository: Preaching focuses predominantly on the text or texts under consideration along with its contexts. Exposition normally concentrates on a single text of scripture but it is sometimes possible for a thematic/theological message or a historical/biographical discourse to be expository in nature.

VII. KEYS TO EFFECTIVE PREACHING

Not all preaching can be classified as successful. Some preaching falls miserably short. Bible preaching should be powerful, penetrating the very heart and spirit of the listener. What are the necessary ingredients to improving our preaching? Here are eight basic ingredients that must be in every message to make it successful preaching (I Cor 2:1-5).

A. Preaching with Edification (I Corinthians 14:3-5,12,17,26; Ephesians 4:12,15,29; I Timothy 1:4; Acts 9:31)

1. Greek: *oikodomeo*
    a. Definition: Home build, construct, rebuild, build up, build together, improvement
    b. Translated in the New Testament: build (25 times), builder (5 times), be in building (1 time), edify (7 times), embolden (1 time).

2. Edification: preaching which increases and strengthens faith and spiritual life (Isaiah 35:3-4)

3. Edification: preaching that praises the people (Acts 27:9,22; *paraineo* "beside praise).

4. Edification: preaching by consoling, encouraging and comforting the flock with well-chosen words and a Christ-like spirit (I Corinthians 14:3; *parakleesis, paramothia*)

George Whitefield

B. Preaching with Revelation (I Corinthians 14:6,26)

   1. Greek (*apokalupsis*): From covering, the unveiling of something to make manifest, lay bare, make visible that which is hidden to the eye. (Galatians 2:2; Ephesians 3:3; 1:17-18; John 16:13)

   2. It carries with it the idea of "something that has been in hiding, buried in the earth, that which has been covered, but now is revealed; one coming forth publicly with his view."

C. Preaching with Inspiration (I Corinthians 14:6)

   1. Prophecy (Gr *propheteia*): A word coming from divine inspiration to declare the mind of God in any situation, to speak as the voice of God.

   2. Inspiration (Gr *theopneustos*): The breath of God specifically placed as the Spirit is the spring of life. Scriptures house divine vitality, the source of life, as contrasted to human writings which neither have nor give life.

   3. Oracle (Gr *logion*): A divinely inspired word filled with the breath of God (I Peter 4:11; Acts 7:38; Romans 3:2; II Samuel 16:23)

   4. Speaking the word of the Lord (II Timothy 4:3; Acts 7:57; I Kings 17:24; 22:14). Sermons are to be reflections, not of our opinions but of our deepest convictions. The preacher's responsibility is to proclaim what we perceive to be the word of God. Anyone bold enough to enter a pulpit to speak for God should hold some strong convictions that have been reached through inward struggle, biblical research, prayer and openness to the Holy Spirit. There are times when the preacher does not speak for the people but to the people. Prophetic preaching at times comes to the people as a challenge, a confrontation, a diagnosis of a spiritual problem with the proper prescription.

D. Preaching with Teaching (I Corinthians 14:6)

   1. Doctrine (Gr *didakee*): Clear, systematic instruction, imparting carefully, slowly, line upon line, gradual, stages, progressively. It comes from the root word that means one who "stands over" such as a superintendent. It is where we get our word "doctor."

   2. Systematic, organized, carefully thought through material that is gradually developed to meet a definite need (Matthew 7:28; 22:33; Mark 1:22; 11:18; Luke 4:32; Acts 13:12).

Empowering Your Preaching

3. Moving the sheep from pasture to pasture systematically and skillfully as a pastor/rancher.

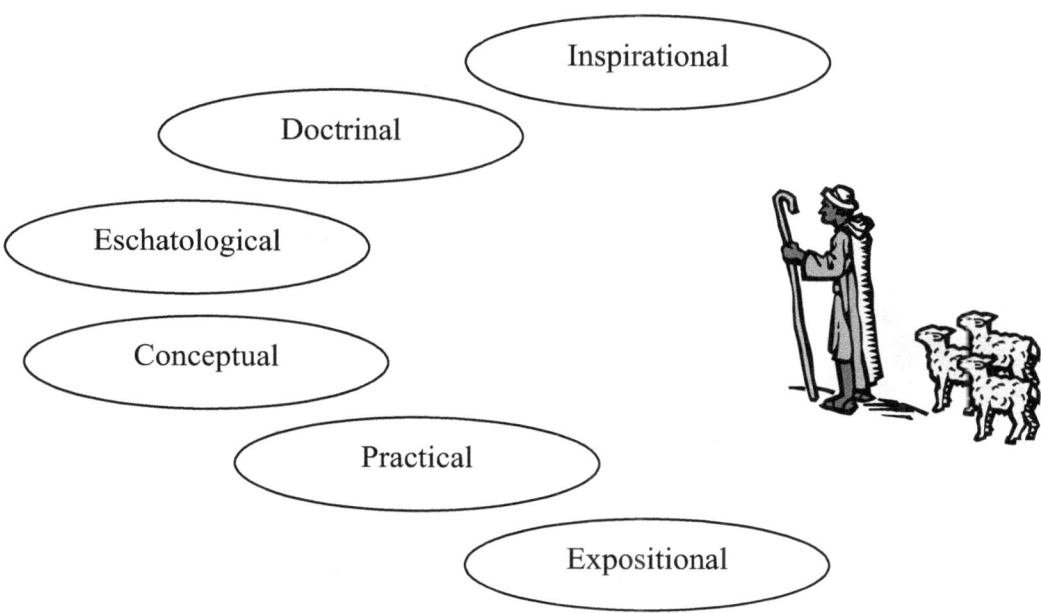

- Inspirational
- Doctrinal
- Eschatological
- Conceptual
- Practical
- Expositional

Empowering Your Preaching

The 32 Proven Laws for the Preacher

1. **The Law of Keeping Your Own Well**
    The preacher's spiritual state will come through the preaching ultimately. You cannot hide an empty spirit with the speaking of many words. Preaching is the act of impartation, not just communication. The preacher must keep his own heart and spirit full of the virtues of God, healthy and growing, vivacious, full of life and all good things. Nothing will keep your well full better than consistent devotional reading of the pure word of God coupled with consistent, Holy Spirit-empowered prayer.

2. **The Law of The Hidden Sermon**
    Whatever is in the sermon will first be in the preacher: clearness, logicalness, sincerity, sweetness or a wrong or wounded spirit. A wounded spirit may result in harshness of spirit, cynical attitude or too apologetic. It is not greatness of spirit that causes us to be critical or harsh, but littleness of spirit. The Preacher should be an able person with a good attitude toward himself and toward the people. Love makes truth palatable. Truth without love could destroy a person by its brutality. Remember, you must love truth but you also must love the people you are preaching to and they must feel this love attitude permeated throughout the preaching.

3. **The Law of Enjoying the Seasons**
    A preacher will have different spiritual seasons that will affect his preaching. When long, unexpected dry periods happen, the preacher may become concerned that he has done something to quench the anointing or that God has withdrawn a measure of anointing without explanation. A preacher must learn how to use the seasons for his benefit in developing the preaching. The season of dryness, victory, sorrow, grief, unsettledness, stretching, discouragement, emptiness and fullness can all be used by the Holy Spirit to bring life and depth to the preacher and the preached word.

4. **The Law of The Abiding Anointing**
    When the preacher lingers too long and too often outside his spiritual gifting and calling, the anointing may decline. Administration, program management, people's problems, too much non-biblical reading or draining activities may quench the preacher's quickened spirit. The signs of inspiration may evaporate and speaking may become more work and less anointing. The preacher must realize that the authority behind preaching resides not in the preacher but in the biblical text, not in emotion but in the Holy Spirit that inspired the text. When you do not feel the anointing, preach on by faith in the word of God. The anointing will be there and affect the people because it abides in the word of God.

5. **The Law of Cultivating a Well-Fed Mind**
    The preacher must continually read and think deeply about a variety of important subjects. Studying for sermons does not necessarily cultivate a well-informed mind. One must read books that expose the preacher to material that stretches the mind and enlarges the vocabulary. The reading of the word of God consistently in different translations will feed the spirit and the mind. Read theological books that challenge your ability to think and reason.

Empowering Your Preaching

6. **The Law of Incarnation Before Proclamation**
Truth must become marinated into the speaker and then transmitted into the people. The word must become incarnated. It is not just good teaching, intellectualism or illustrations but incarnation. Preaching is the ministry of the word in your life extended to the people. As the preacher grows, so grows the message and so grows the church. It is easier to make a sermon of the letter, out of skill and study, than to grow a sermon in the depths of the preacher's spirit. A sermon that arises out of the inner life will touch the inner life of others.

7. **The Law of Knowing Hidden Danger Zones**
Beware of preaching from the pulpit to correct a particular problem, person or activity or of preaching when you are in a bad mood or critical about something going on in the church. A danger zone can also be fatigue. When the preacher goes to the pulpit with tired emotions, a fatigued mind and a dose of discouragement, he may see and say things he was not intending to see or say. A fatigued preacher may also be more apt to weep and be apologetic or weep and be condemning, harsh, or a little sharp in spirit and attitude.

8. **The Law of Discretion With Illustration and Stories**
The rule to follow is that an illustration should illustrate the truth, not elevate the preacher. Why am I using this? To illustrate a point? To elevate my standing? To identify with the people? We must connect abstract truth to human condition; real life illustrations help us to apply truth. Use your imagination. This is the faculty of making something new out of that which is old. Learn how to say things in a more interesting way. The relationship of seasonings and sauces to gourmet cooking parallels the role of introductions, illustrations and conclusions.

9. **The Law of Passion**
The preacher must be a heart person in the pulpit with a strong passion for God, the message and the people. To preach with passion is to preach with energy and emotion, convincing with power. Passion moves people. Passion is showing deep feelings about the subject at hand. The ability to communicate the depth of those feelings is true preaching. Charles Spurgeon exhorted on keeping your preaching alive and passionate, "I dread getting to be a mere preaching machine without my heart and soul being exercised in this solemn duty, lest it should be a mere piece of clockwork." Big hearts make big preachers. The preacher binds the people to him by his heart, not his head. People may admire gifts and abilities but they will be affected by the passion of the preacher's heart.

10. **The Law of Knowing When to Stop**
The length of the sermon will vary depending on the speaker, the audience, the event, the culture or the country. The preacher must learn to recognize that "now" is the time to stop. The wise preacher will not complain about the lack of time or waste time on things of lesser importance. Abandon the low-priority items in the message and focus on the most important matters. A sermon does not have to be eternal to be immortal. There ought to be such simplicity that all ages will enjoy and understand the one main thrust of the message.

Empowering Your Preaching

11. **The Law of Connecting Individually and Powerfully**
    The preacher must establish rapport quickly and keep it during the whole message delivery. Connecting to a congregation should first be seen as connecting to a person, for preaching is very much just that—connecting one person at a time. The connecting happens through the preacher's attitude, voice tones, mannerisms, sincerity of thought and action, openness, realness, person to person attitude. It is not under the people or over the people but with the people. Connecting is the sacred bond that grows between a preacher and a congregation. It is indescribable when you have it and utterly horrible when you don't.

12. **The Law of Finishing Strong**
    The introduction to any message is of prime importance. The content will determine quality and longevity of effect, but the conclusion will determine the impact and the people's response. The conclusion to the message should be prepared carefully. This includes both your final statements and the song that will accentuate the atmosphere you anticipate will be present at your conclusion. Be bold. Call for response. Be specific. The word has been preached; believe that people are ready to respond. This is the part of the sermon most likely to be neglected. Just as athletes need to finish strong at the end of a race or game, so the preacher must be at his best in the closing minutes.

13. **The Law of Deep Penetration**
    The preacher must have patience and faith in the power of preaching the word of God. The word of God is likened to a seed and it takes time for a seed to germinate, grow and produce fruit. God's word is never wasted and it will not return void. It will penetrate the hardest heart. It takes faith to believe it is going deep. The word of God is a two-edged sword that pierces even to the dividing asunder of the soul and spirit, the joints and marrow. The words of the preacher will be sharp, pointed, powerful, penetrating quickly and deeply.

14. **The Law of Guarding Your Emotions**
    Your present emotional condition can affect your preaching. Self-control is of necessity. The whole of the preacher's personality must be involved in the preaching: body, soul and spirit. The Apostle Paul preached with tears, deep emotions and with a mighty intellect. We need to use our emotions, but to do so with wisdom and Holy Spirit control. Spurgeon once commented on dry preachers who show no emotion, "He would make a good martyr. He was so dry he would burn well."

15. **The Law of Careful Vulnerability**
    The preacher can use personal experience to reflect on the fact that we all have common struggles. You are saying, "I am human. I've been there. I understand." People today have come to expect personal preaching, vulnerability and self-revelation. Being conscious and aware of our own inadequacy and weakness, we discover the power of God in the word of truth. Our confessions or transparency with people must bring them to the word of truth. There are things that are best left out when being vulnerable. Being honest and open does not mean being unwise, rude, crude, or too personal on sensitive issues.

Empowering Your Preaching

16. **The Law of Using the Right Words**
    The preacher will need to be diligent in searching for the right words to clothe truth in. The careful preacher will use his dictionary of synonyms and will keep in mind Mark Twain's dictum that the difference between any word and the right word is the difference between lightning and a lightning bug. The preacher is a craftsman and words are his tools. The right word for the right thought will have greater impact than a wrong word or an acceptable word. Winston Churchill's famous declaration about the Royal Air Force in 1941 is a classic use of the impact of a few words, "Never in the field of human conflict was so much owed by so many to so few."

17. **The Law of Resilience**
    The preacher can encounter satanic attacks through circumstances, satanic harassment, and unnatural amounts of accusation, criticism and questioning of motives. Fear and loss of confidence may become apparent, causing the preacher to question his calling, his giftedness, his placement or his own heart. The preacher must continually encourage himself in the Lord and have a great "come back" spirit week after week. The preacher must know how to return to the wellsprings of his calling. The holy oil that has been given freely in the past is still present and permanent. Encourage yourself in the Lord. Taking time to pray and plan your preaching by using break times when you are not under the pressure of preaching every week will serve you in planning ahead.

18. **The Law of Planning**
    The preacher need not waste time agonizing over every message if he would plan ahead by season or by specific needs in the church. The Spirit of God can break in at any time and change your plans, giving you a specific message for a specific time. Series preaching is one way to plan your preaching calendar.

19. **The Law of The Right Timing**
    The preacher must know when a God-thought has matured enough for it to become a message to preach. The message may have many undeveloped parts and need time to develop. The preacher must keep putting the material into the oven over and over again until it is cooked and ready to serve. Know the right timing to preach a God-thought. Avoid pre-planned calendar preaching outlines. These can look good on paper but have no life to them.

20. **The Law of The Critic's Help**
    The preacher cannot preach without a certain level of criticism from those he preaches to and from other preachers. Criticism can have a devastating effect upon the spirit and attitude of the preacher if he has not determined his response to criticism before receiving it. Respond graciously, honestly and briefly. Never respond immediately. Let your emotions settle down and let the Holy Spirit have a chance to reveal truth.

21. **The Law of "Your Style is the Best Style"**
    Every preacher is unique and must develop his/her own style out of his own uniqueness of personality, mental capacity and spiritual gifting. Be yourself, your best self, and let the Holy Spirit put the imprint of your life on the message. Trevor Davies, the great Welsh preacher, said "I was never so consciously a complete failures as when I tried to imitate someone else."

Empowering Your Preaching

22. **The Law of Enlarging Your Capacity**
    Broad education is important for the preacher: theology, history, culture, philosophy, linguistics, communication skills are all part of the total treasure chest he will draw from. Never be satisfied with your preaching. You can always grow. Success can become a great enemy of progress. The preacher must never believe everything people say about his preaching. A lazy preacher is doomed to limit his full capacity and rob the people of God. Keep growing at all costs. Grow, enlarge, read, pray, listen. Never stop learning.

23. **The Law of Simplicity That Always Works**
    There is power and authority in being simple, precise and to the point. The preacher must avoid complexity which breeds levels of confusion. Simplicity allows for the listener to remember and apply what is being preached. It is better that people grasp hold of one or two simple, direct thoughts than to be overwhelmed in a maze of points.

24. **The Law of Impartation**
    The preacher must have something to impart before impartation can take place. The process involves both the substance or content that is to be imparted as well as the spirit and zeal of the imparter. The preacher must not b detached from the truth he wishes to impart. It must be in him, on him, around him and flow from his mind, will and emotions. The preacher must be totally immersed in the truth and he must impart with faith, confidence and enthusiasm. He must impart, not clinically or academically, but spiritually.

25. **The Law of Spirit-Driven Speaking**
    The preacher must have the element of freedom, flow and spontaneity in the message delivery. He must be open to the influence and power of the Holy Spirit to direct his thoughts and, at times, not be tied to the message which has been carefully prepared. He must preach with demonstration of the spirit and of power, not only in word but in the Holy Spirit. Be open to the inspiration of the moment. Some of the best things a preacher says may not be premeditated or written out in the sermon material.

26. **The Law of Strategic Humor**
    It is hard to engage the emotions of a congregation, but once you engage any emotion it is relatively easy to enlist the other emotions. Humor can be dangerous. Don't put people down. Laugh at yourself. The preacher should be a serious and sober person with a serious and sober challenge—the changing of people for all eternity. The preacher should never give the impression that preaching is something light, superficial or trivial. Warren Wiersbe states, "If the preacher has a sense of humor, he had better dedicate it to the Lord and let the Spirit direct him in its use. For true humor can become a toy to play with, a tool to build with or a dangerous weapon to fight with."

27. **The Law of Preciseness**
    It is easy for a preacher to make things sound better than they really are as we relate experiences, events, turning point spiritual crises, family devotions and more. It is important to be precise, to the point and exacting. Be specific in Bible references, quotations, dates, articles and facts of any kind. Footnote the source of quotes or statistics in your message. Ask your wife or children if the recounting of an event was exactly the way it happened.

Empowering Your Preaching

28. **The Law of Fresh Manna**
Our preaching can become lazy. We can live off yesterday's manna and keep bringing out the "golden oldies." Slothful sermonizing begins with riding on our talent or gift of speaking rather than a word from God. Our preaching can be shallow with lack of thought. It can be a commentary into the obvious with careless content and vague application. These all reflect little preparation. Preaching should be interesting, alive, fresh and enjoyable, even when uncomfortable.

29. **The Law of Proper Use of Modern Technology**
Drama, PowerPoint, video. Drama should be used as an appropriate way to impart the main truth of your message. It is not for entertainment, not for humor only, but to drive home the point of the message. Whatever value media and modern technology may have, their impact and effectiveness are measured by whether the message has penetrated the hearts of people by the power of the Holy Spirit.

30. **The Law of The Present Tense**
People do not usually desire to hear about things that happened 4,000 years ago unless there is a present tense application. A preacher that lingers in the past tense too long will run the risk of losing the people's interest and missing the mark of preaching—changed lives. The purpose of preaching is to discover the timeless truths and principles within the word of God, clothe them in 21st century language and apply them to the needs of present tense people. The preacher must take ancient material and make relevant messages.

31. **The Law of The Personal Touch**
Preaching is best when the preacher has learned what is called the "I-Thou" relationship, you and the person in the congregation. You must set up a sense of you speaking to them one-on-one, giving them a sense of personal rapport. Use "you" and "I" rather than "me". Avoid the impersonal abstract of "someone said", "they", or "people think". Speak to the person as if you were alone with them. A young lad, hearing Spurgeon preach, turned to his mother and remarked, "That man is talking to me." At times I will say to the congregation, "Pull up your chair, put on the coffee and slip on your comfortable shoes. I want to spend a half-hour with you this morning." Lean over the pulpit and say something like, "Here we are again to talk about what is going on in your soul and mine."

32. **The Law of Prayer-Filled Preaching**
The preacher who learns the place of prayer in the preparation of the sermon and the delivery will be a more impacting preacher. If the preacher is to deliver God's message with power, prayer must permeate his life and furnish a Holy Spirit environment for the Holy Spirit to work in and through. Prayer in the secret place makes preaching powerful in the public place. Prayer is indispensable in biblical preaching. Prayer saturates the preacher with God's presence. It saturates the words, the notes, and the people. The whole process from God-thought to God-word to God-message must be saturated with prayer. E.M. Bounds wrote, "Light praying will make light preaching. Prayer makes preaching strong and makes it stick."

"If then you are wise, you will show yourself rather as a reservoir than as a waterpipe. For a pipe spreads abroad water as it receives it, but a reservoir waits until it is filled to overflowing and thus communicates without loss to itself its superabundant water."

Empowering Your Preaching

The Preacher's God-Thought to God-Message

The preparing of sermons is very personal and what works for one person does not always work for another. There are certain obvious elements to all sermons: study, organization and communication are usually involved. After thirty years of preaching, I seek to offer some personal illustrations as to my process from the God-thought to the preaching of the message.

I. **STEP ONE: DISCERNING THE GOD THOUGHT**
   I Corinthians 11:23; Galatians 1:12; Isaiah 33:18; Proverbs 2:1

   This is usually the most work, yet at times it comes quickly and out of nowhere. Charles Spurgeon said, "I confess that I frequently sit hour after hour praying and waiting for a subject and that this is the main part of my study."[1]

   > "The preparation of sermons involves sweat and labor and is extremely difficult at times."
   > (Martyn Lloyd Jones)

   A. **The Prayer and Worship Atmosphere**
      I have always enjoyed an atmosphere that results in the stirring of my own spirit toward God and the word. Prayer intermingled with worship music allows for the Spirit of God to move upon the mind and heart, preparing myself like a plowed field ready to receive the seed of the word. This could be done quickly or could be a season of time given to waiting on the Lord. The God-thought must grow out of the soil of your soul and its roots must come from deep within your own experience and your ability to hear the spirit and receive from God's written word.

   B. **The Prophetic or Rhema Word**
      I believe in the written word of God as the basis for all preaching and teaching: the logos word, unchanging, trustworthy, always there. I also believe in the rhema word that arises out of the written word. The rhema word as defined by Vine's Dictionary is exemplified in the injunction to take the sword of the Spirit which is the word of God. Here the reference is not the whole Bible as such, but to the individual scripture which the Spirit brings to our remembrance for use in time of need. A prerequisite to this is the regular storing of the mind with scripture. I find rhema words come to me out of meditating on certain portions of the word: at times one word or a phrase or a story or an event. This starts me on a journey of seeking God and asking for illumination.

   C. **The God-Thought Kept in Store**
      I have found over the years there are many God-thoughts that come to me but I lose them because I don't write them down. A good discipline is to keep a "God-Thought" journal. You don't have to worry about what the God-thought means or try to develop each one as they come, but simply put them into your treasure chest and wait for the right timing. I have God-thoughts that I have kept for literally years without developing them and yet, when the seed is taken out of the box and planted, it brings forth fresh fruit immediately.

Empowering Your Preaching

    D.   **The Burden of the Lord**
Throughout scripture we read about those who received the burden of the Lord and form that burden they developed a God-thought, a God-word for their day. Many times my God-thought begins as a spiritual burden, something God puts into my spirit through spiritual experiences, observations, crises, problems, living life in a pressure cooker. The burden could be something God is dealing with me about: a sin, a short-coming, a need in my own life or ministry, a realization of spiritual conflict or a burden for some person, a need in our church congregation that is not so obvious to others but has become a burden to me.

II.   **STEP TWO: DEVELOPING THE GOD-THOUGHT**
This is not a subjective process but a definite building block approach to the developing of the God-thought into a "word or a message", a biblical and practical way for the hearers to understand the word. The developing of the God-thought can actually go several ways, depending on the nature of the God-thought: thematic, theological, historical or biographical.

    A.   **The God-Thought Developed by Systematic Research**
If I have received a biblical word as part of my God-thought, then I will begin with a word study on that particular word. For example, if the God-thought is found within the word "first", then I would go to my concordance and lay out a word study on "first", possibly finding other synonyms for first and looking them up as well. I'm not going to try to interpret my God-thought before I finish my ground word. First I must finish with the word study and compile it into some order that will serve me in my preparing the God-thought. Obviously you must know how to do a word study in order to achieve this first step. The God-thought may be best developed from a portion of scripture, a verse, chapter or a whole book of the Bible. If this be the case, I will need to do exegesis of the scriptures and build on biblical research. Exegesis deals with the original languages of scripture (Hebrew and Greek) and builds on sound hermeneutical principles.

    B.   **The God-Thought Study Processed and Structured**
This is not an outline I will preach from but an outline that organizes my potential thoughts about the God-word which I am now seeing a little more clearly. As I have processed the God-thought through a word, passage or some kind of word study I have found some key passages, key stories, or key characters that could be easily used to develop a message around. My study will be put into an organized outline which allows me quick access to the biblical breadth of the subject. The God-thought may be developed as a word study, character study, place study or an expositional study of scripture.

    C.   **The God-Thought Zeroed In On and Narrowed**
This is one of the hardest steps because the preacher has many thoughts by now, not only the original God-thought but also other quickened words that have surfaced along the way. If the preacher is not careful, he/she will end up chasing many words and either end up frustrated or losing the God-thought in the ever-widening breadth of research. At this point, choose to narrow your approach to a specific passage, a specific historical event or a specific character. If my God-thought is around the word "first" and I have thirty scriptures to choose from, I need to narrow my approach quickly and go on to my next step. At this point, I will make my first outline draft to aid me in narrowing and organizing my approach.

Empowering Your Preaching

III. STEP THREE: DEVELOPING THE GOD-THOUGHT INTO A STUDY OUTLINE

A. The Study Outline as a Compass

I now move on to the actual message development work with confidence and a sense of having a track to follow. I'm not double-minded about the direction I should take in developing my message and I'm not tempted to go into other interesting areas of study. I am focused and I have a study compass to follow—my message outline. With the message study outline, I can actually save time by working only on the areas within my study outline. I know what to do. If I take a side trip, I can easily get back on track. My research can now get serious. I begin with the first part of the study outline, usually definitions.

> **Message Outline Sample**
>
> I. Defining the Word First
> Dictionaries
> Hebrew and Greek
> Other Sources
>
> II. The First Things of Jesus
>   I narrow my approach to only use the Gospels
>   In the gospels, I focus on only the "first things" of Jesus

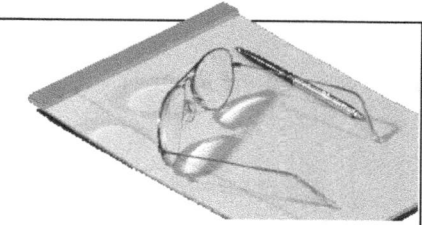

B. The Work of Research and Definitions

The work of research will depend upon the kind of message I am developing. An expository message will demand different study techniques than a word study based message or a character study based message. If I choose the word "first" as the foundation to my message, then I would need to do a word study, find definitions and groupings of scriptures and thoughts on 'first." Following my study outline, I research Hebrew and Greek dictionaries as well as any other sources to help define my key word. Following my study outline, I see the word "first" must be narrowed to the first things of Jesus. I then choose seven key scriptures to work on and I develop each scripture into a main point.

Scriptures of the Seven Firsts of Jesus

1. Mt 6:33 But *seek first* the kingdom of God and His righteousness, and all these things shall be added to you.
2. Mt 5:24-25 Leave your gift there before the altar, and go your way. *First be reconciled* to your brother, and then come and offer your gift. Agree with your adversary quickly, while you are on the way with him, lest your adversary deliver you to the judge, the judge hand you over to the officer, and you are thrown into prison.
3. Mt 7:4-5 How can you say to your brother, 'Let me remove the speck from your eye'; and look, a plank is in your own eye? Hypocrite! *First remove the plank* from your own eye, and then you will see clearly to remove the speck out of your brother's eye.
4. Mt 12:29 Or how can one enter a strong man's house and plunder his goods, unless he *first binds the strong man*? And then he will plunder his house.
5. Mt 22:36-38 Teacher, which is the great commandment in the law? Jesus said to him," 'You shall love the Lord your God with all your heart, with all your soul, and with all your mind.' "This is the *first and great commandment.*
6. Mt 23:26 Blind Pharisee, *first cleanse the inside* of the cup and dish, that the outside of them may be clean also.
7. Mt 28:1 Now after the Sabbath, as the *first day of the week* began to dawn, Mary Magdalene and the other Mary came to see the tomb.

Empowering Your Preaching

C. The Layered Research of Each Part of the Study Outline

Now that I have a set outline and my main key words have been researched, I can move on to researching each main section of my message. This is done keeping the main purpose of the message in the forefront of my mind at all times. I add to these points from other resources, commentaries, dictionaries and articles pertaining to the subject at hand. It is wise to do what I call "layered research," covering each section of the message with a first layer of research and then go back and add another layer as you have time. If you don't have a plan, you may spend all your time researching the first point and create an imbalanced message. Research the whole message generally before going deep on any one point.

IV. STEP FOUR: DEVELOPING THE GOD-THOUGHT INTO A MESSAGE OUTLINE

A. The Introduction of the Message

By definition, to "introduce" means to acquaint or to bring into play for the first time. Most of the time my introduction and title of the message demand my full attention and at times can take concentrated time to develop. I write the introduction out in one or two brief paragraphs, stating precisely what the listener can expect from this message and challenging some aspect of their heart to intently listen to the forthcoming message. I always start with two or three key passages (if my message is thematic). The congregation reads them out loud in one translation (usually written out on a Power Points presentation) so as to bring unity of focus. I then proceed to a short, interesting story, statistics, illustrations, questions to ponder or a real life "Frank Damazio" experience. By now I have the listener's full attention and they know what I am speaking on, why I am speaking on this subject and how they will benefit greatly from this message. John Henry Jowett said, "I have a conviction that no sermon is ready for preaching until we can express its theme in a short, pregnant sentence as clear as crystal."

First Things of Jesus

Putting first things first is an issue at the heart of life. All of us feel torn by the things we want to do, by the demands placed on us, by the many responsibilities we have. Many people today could and do feel disoriented or confused. We may have no real sense of: What are the "first things"? What are the "first" and most important things in my life? Where do I find what is important? What should be my "first things" to live by?

Jesus gives us the wisdom for a life worth living. Jesus is able to summarize for us all of His teachings by using one word: first. Jesus summarizes what is the most important of all His parables, doctrines and stories by giving us seven firsts to live by. He boiled it down, distilled thousands of teachings, writings and theories into the one word: first. If we could grasp our core values, they would save us years of doubts, confusion and misplaced energy. We would live a life with direction and satisfaction If you want to be happy, do these things. Just as Nike was able to boil it down and pare things down to this essence: Just do it!

Empowering Your Preaching

B. **The Main Body of the Message**

The introduction now given, I move on to the main body of my message. My habit is to preach from an outline of usually three to five main points. The first step is to form a general outline of the subject. At this stage, I am not concerned with how the outline is worded or if there is a rhythm to the thoughts, but I simply focus on the main points of the message.

After that is done, I begin the fine touches on the specific preaching outline. Techniques that I use are alliteration with each main point beginning with a specific letter and rhythmic phrasing in which each phrase has the same "feel" to it. The goal is to have points that are easily understood, pleasant to listen to and easy to remember. Out comes my thesaurus as I search for words that go together. This can take one or two hours in itself if I am going to perfect my sermon outline.

After I perfect my introduction and my preaching outline feels right, I go back through the whole message again to add another layer with more supporting scriptures. Organization in a sermon must be a servant and not a master. The tension of form and function is always present.

1. First seek the kingdom of God: *Renewing Kingdom lifestyle* (Mt 6:33)
2. First be reconciled with your brother: *Repairing faulty relationships* (Mt 5:24-25)
3. First remove the log from your own eye: *Removing judgmental attitudes* (Mt 7:4-5)
4. First bind the strong man: *Recovering stolen goods* (Mt 12:29)
5. First the greatest commandment: *Reviving passion for God* (Mt 22:36-38)
6. First cleanse the inside of the cup: *Renouncing destructive sins* (Mt 23:26)
7. First day of the week began to dawn: *Respecting the Lord's Day* (Mt 28:1; Heb 10:25)

C. **The Stories and Illustrations for the Message**

The stories and illustrations used to make a message impacting and living must be carefully planned by the preacher. This is as much work as the whole process of researching and preparing the message material. The preacher should have a treasure chest filled with great stories and illustrations and a quick way to access this material. There are many books as well as Internet websites which a preacher can acquire to find stories and illustrations. If done wisely and tastefully, one of the best ways to illustrate is to use personal, real life stories. It is always better to ask first if possible. The story or illustration should be thought out and placed into the message outline at the appropriate spot. Think through the emotion you are interjecting into the message as well as how you will exit the story without losing the message momentum. A story or illustration should be kept in hand as to how much time will be spent and how much intensity. It is easy to get carried away with stories or illustrations. Remember, the word is the central part of the message. The word of God will change lives. Stories or illustrations must support the word, not distract from it.

Empowering Your Preaching

D.   The Conclusion to the Message

The conclusion of the message should be carefully thought through, prayed through and talked through. I will preach the whole message to myself on "fast forward", seeking to get the total impact of the message and how best to bring it to a conclusion. Ending, bringing it to a close and shutting up all describe what I must accomplish. I must bring the listener to a decision and apply the message. I personally like to end my message with a definite goal in mind, a response to the word that is direct, brief, bold and Holy Spirit driven. Altar calls are awkward for some preachers. Embarrassment because of little response from the congregation may cause some to not ask for a response. The plea could be for salvation, prodigals, healing, help, encouragement, and prayer of agreement. Whatever the purpose, do it with faith and directness. Know what you want to accomplish. Prepare your words carefully in your message notes and then launch out. God will help you. The Holy Spirit will confirm His word. God has already prepared people for your message.

"To me, the work of preaching is the highest and greatest and the most glorious calling to which anyone can be called."
(Martyn Lloyd-Jones)

Empowering Your Preaching

Endnotes

[1] John Wesley, Preface to Sermons on Several Occasion, 1746, from The Works of John Wesley 1, 104-6. Conrad Archer; Bishop, Texas.

[2] Ralph W. Harris, ed. *The New Testament Study Bible Hebrews-Jude.* Springfield, MO: The Complete Biblical Library, 1986. Page 53.

[3] Ralph W. Harris, ed. *The New Testament Study Bible Hebrews-Jude.* Springfield, MO: The Complete Biblical Library, 1986. Page 53.

[4] Harris, page 53.

[5] Harris, page 54.

[6] Charles Spurgeon. *Lectures to My Students.* Pg. 73.

Pictures are from the General Board of Global Ministries. They are from the United Methodist Church's "Wesley's and Their Times" web site, http://gbgm-umc.org/umhistory/wesley

Gaining A Biblical Perspective On Preaching

I Timothy 3:1,17; II Timothy 2:9; 2:15; 4:2

INTRODUCTION

Preaching is a dynamic experience involving the preacher, congregation, message and setting, demanding total dedication of physical, spiritual and intellectual powers plus the presence of the Holy Spirit. Preaching, in the sense that we understand the word (interpreting the will of God through explanation and interpretation of biblical facts), came into Judaism with Ezra and Nehemiah about the 5th century.

I. HEBREW DEFINITIONS

A. Gara = Enunciation of a specific message with specific recipients with an intent to elicit a specific response. This word denotes a planned encounter wherein the subject intentionally confronts the object with a planned message. To meet by appointment."

B. Basar = "To bring news, especially pertaining to military encounters." The concept here is the messenger fresh from the field of battle as the heart of this Hebrew word.

II. GREEK DEFINITIONS

A. Declaim (*apophthenggomai*)

1. Translated in King James Version as:
    a. Say (1)
    b. Speak forth (1)
    c. Utterance (1)

2. Definition: To speak loudly and rhetorically in a lofty voice, with influence and persuasion. (Acts 2:4,14; 26:25)

B. Declare (*ereo*)

1. Translated in King James as:
    a. Call (1)
    b. Say (57)
    c. Speak (9)
    d. Tell (4)

2. Definition: To speak forcefully...a gushing forth. The result is rhema (same root). To make clearly known; to say positively or emphatically... to show or reveal.

Empowering Your Preaching

C. Herald (*kerusso*)

1. Translated in King James:
   a. Preach (53)
   b. Preacher (1)
   c. Proclaim (2)
   d. Publish (5)

2. Definition: To make known publicly, with authority beforehand, literally "proclaim." To proclaim or announce significant news of something to come, as a forerunner. (Mt 3:1; 4:17; 10:7,27; 24:14; Mk 1:4; 16:15; etc.)

D. Heralding (*kerugma*)

1. Translated eight times in the King James as "preaching".

2. Definition: That which is promulgated by a herald or public crier. The message or proclamation by the heralds of God or Christ. The proclamation of the necessity of repentance and reformation made by the Prophetic Jonah (Thayer). (Matthew 12:41; Luke 11:32; Romans 16:25; I Corinthians 1:21; 2:4; 15:14; II Timothy 4:17; Titus 1:3)

E. Evangelize (*euanggelizo*)

1. Definition: To evangelize or bring the evangel.

2. Used in the New Testament
   a. Phillip evangelized with the Word (Act 8:4).
   b. Paul was to be evangelizing among the nations. (Galatians 1:16).

F. Evangelist (*euangelizo*)

1. Sense of bringing "news of victory" or "declaring a victory." Same idea as from the Hebrew word "basar." The messenger comes from the place of battle and declares victory over the enemies or the death of the opponent. (Isaiah 40:10; Psalm 68:11; Isaiah 52:7)

2. The Greek usage and meaning is with full authority and power. Preaching should be accompanied by signs and wonders. They belong together for the Word is powerful and effective! (Mt 4:23; 9:35; 11:5; Lk 9:6; Acts 8:4-8; 10:36; etc.)

G. Announce (*katanggello*)

1. Translated in King James
   a. Declare (2)
   b. Preach (10)
   c. Shew (3)
   d. Speak of (1)
   e. Teach (1)

2. Definition: To declare publicly, to give formal notice.

Empowering Your Preaching

3. Used in the New Testament
   a. Prophets announced these days. (Acts 3:24)
   b. Barnabas and Saul announced the Word. (Acts 13:5; 15:36; 17:13)
   c. The Lord prescribes that those who announce the evangel should be living of the evangel. (I Corinthians 9:14)

H. Charge (*paraggello*)

1. Translated in King James:
   a. Charge (6)
   b. Command (20)
   c. Declare (1)

2. Used in the New Testament
   a. Christ charged His disciples. (Matthew 10:5)
   b. He charged the unclean spirit. (Luke 8:29)
   c. God charged the disciples to herald to the people to certify that Christ was specific to be Judge of the living and the dead. (Acts 10:42)
   d. Paul charged the python spirit to leave the woman. (Acts 16:18)

I. Inform (*anaggello*)

1. The Holy Spirit will inform the disciples. (John 16:13-15)

2. Paul and Barnabas informed the church. (Acts 14:23; 15:4)

J. Publish (*diaggello*)

1. Translated in King James:
   a. Declare (1)
   b. Preach (1)
   c. Signify (1)

2. Definition: To make known publicly.

3. Used in the New Testament:
   a. Publish the kingdom of God. (Luke 9:60)
   b. The Lord's name to be published. (Romans 9:17)

K. Report (*apaggello*)

Definition: To give an account of, as something seen or investigated. A presentation of facts or the record of something. (Mark 6:30; Luke 8:47; Acts 4:23; I Corinthians 14:25)

Empowering Your Preaching

III. SUMMARIZING BIBLICAL PREACHING

A. It is not just a talk. The preacher preaches to produce results. He is there to influence people, to do something to those people. He is there to deal with the whole person.

B. It is a transaction between the preacher and the listener. He deals with sin and life in a vital and radical manner. He transmits something and, because of the Spirit of God, they receive something.

C. It is not just the imparting of academic or organized thoughts of knowledge into the listener.

D. It is that which deals with the total person. The hearer becomes involved and knows that he has been dealt with and addressed by God through the preacher, something has taken place in the hearer that will affect his total life.

E. According to Martin Lloyd Jones, "My true definition of preaching must say that man is there to deliver the message of God, a message from God to those people, an ambassador." Preaching is not so much speaking about God as the preacher is the vessel through whom God Himself is speaking.

F. It is more than form. Form must not become more important than substance. Oratory and eloquence must not become the essence of preaching. Preaching then becomes only a form of unprofitable entertainment, a kind of showmanship, small talk, and rhetoric.

G. Preaching is the ministry of the word in your life extended to the people. Preaching is not just a science or an art. The style of preaching is not the measuring rod for biblical preaching. Truth must become marinated in the speaker and then transmitted into the people. The word must become incarnated. It is not just good teaching, intellectualism or illustration but incarnation. (Titus 1:1,3)

Empowering Your Preaching

History of Preaching

Apostolic 4-69	Preaching of Jesus and the Apostles Proclamation of the Word with power, followed by signs and wonders The supernatural
Patristic 70-430	From about 70-300 it was the laymen preaching, nonprofessional, untrained and yet had a great impact upon the world. From 300-430 there was a remarkable rise in the power of preaching. Within the Church, more form in sermons, a finished canon, more biblical preaching, more orderly worship service, stability in doctrine and the culture. The training of preachers added power to the pulpit. People loved oratory and education. Basil the Great, Gregory of Nyssa, Chrysostom, Ambrose, Augustine, Polycarp-Bishop of Smyrna (68-160), Ignatious-Bishop of Antioch (30-110), Clement-Bishop of Rome (50-100)
Early Medieval 430-1095	The decay of preaching founded in the word or preaching with power was all but destroyed. Preachers became corrupt; liturgy strangled the power of the pulpit. Preacher became priest; doctrines were corrupted. Allegorizing was rampant. 476 Fall of Rome: period of decay, decline and hopelessness. Preaching was affected by this event; Augustine's "City of God". During this period the Papacy was finally established. Gregory the Great (590-604) established Catholic ceremony, chanting, Latin used, purgatory, rise in monasticism, no real preaching to the people from the Bible. 7th-11th centuries considered the Dark Ages of preaching.
Central Medieval 1095-1361	Age of scholasticism ushered in new concern for learning. Mysticism was strong. Preaching became popular again. Period of great cathedrals, clergy ranked top of the social order. Intellectualism was on the rise with the founding of many universities. Great crowds gathered to hear preaching which was given with dramatic presentations. Expository methods used. Francis of Assisi, Dominic.
Reformation 1361-1572	Two distinct periods—Renaissance 1361-1499 and Reformation 1500-1572 The renaissance was a time of new thinking, new art, new attitudes. Classical scholarship, intellectual interest, philosophy, independent of theology. Translation of Bible into English in 1382 by John Wycliffe. Martin Luther (1517) 93 theses against the Catholic Church Luther Germany; Calvin—France; Zwingli—Zurich; Knox--Scotland The development of printing brought the most influence in this age. 1446 John Gutenberg, invention of printing press, moveable type. Preaching was revived. Biblical preaching was at its height.
Early Modern 1572-1789	John & Charles Wesley and George Whitfield formed a team of preachers called "The Great Awakening." Evangelistic movement known as "pietism." Known as the golden age of preaching. Age of literary giants: John Bunyan, Shakespeare. Preaching was once again mainly verse by verse exposition. Church services continued for hours with heavy context. Greek/Latin flowed profoundly. Homiletics became the form of preaching. Many books written on preaching. The beginnings of the natural style of preaching, less artificial style.
Later Modern 1789-1900	Influence of international, national and religious pressures. Unemployment, riots, telephone, socialism, Karl Marx, industrialization, urbanization. Time of great pressure, but also time of great preaching. Revivals of Finney, Moody, gave way to Bible conferences, YMCA, Salvation Army birthed. Church membership declined. Rise in biblical criticism, liberalism. Science became number one, replacing religion, stressing self-sufficiency. Preaching method was topical rather than expository. Nearly 2/3 of all preachers were students of Hebrew, Greek, Latin. Great missionary age.
Contemporary 1900-present	World War I/World War II and the Great Depression. Darwin's evolution became prominent. Existentialism became world view of philosophy. Henry Drummond, Henry Ward Beecher challenged the decay. The new technology came in, influence of scientific thought, higher criticism, materialism, psychology that ignored the fall of man, spirit of liberalism, questioning inspiration of Bible, virgin birth, deity. Age of Bible translations: RV/NAS, Moffat, Goodspeed. 1905-1930 time of much church construction in suburbs. Preaching declined in context, many popular approaches to preaching, poor quality, little.

Teaching the Church How to Listen

INTRODUCTION
A good listener is a prepared listener. His mind is ready to receive by giving of his attention one hundred percent. He then receives the vital message through an act of the Spirit as He ministers truth to the listener's innermost being, allowing him to hear with his spiritual ears. Hunger and a desire to understand the Word and preparation spiritually through prayer are key elements in the making of a good listener.

I. **NEHEMIAH AND EZRA: FEASTS OF TABERNACLES**

    A.   Reading the Book of the Law: Israel's Bible
        1.   Deuteronomy 31:24
        2.   Deuteronomy 32:1-2
        3.   Nehemiah 8:1-2

    B.   Reading the Bible
        1.   Psalm 119:161
        2.   Bible in 1100 languages
        3.   Bible is the book of God

II. **SEVEN ATTITUDES CONCERNING THE WORD OF GOD**

    A.   The Attitude of Hunger for the Word (Nehemiah 8:1; I Peter 2:2)

    B.   The Attitude of Desiring Understanding (Nehemiah 8:2,9,12-13)

        1.   Revelation, inspiration and illumination
            a.   Revelation = Receiving truth
            b.   Inspiration = Recording truth
            c.   Illumination = Understanding truth

        2.   By understanding the house is established (Proverbs 24:3)

        3.   Understanding must be enlightened (Ephesians 1:18; I Samuel 14:27-28; Psalm 19:10; I Corinthians 10:1; I Corinthians 12:1; Romans 1:13)

        4.   Understanding must be opened (Luke 24:45)

    C.   The Attitude of Attentiveness and Interest (Nehemiah 8:3)

    Ears were attentive
    1.   Uncircumcised ears (Jeremiah 6:10)
    2.   Stubborn ears (Zechariah 7:8-14)
    3.   Dull of hearing (Hebrews 5:11; 6:11-12)
    4.   Opened ears (Isaiah 50:4-5)

Empowering Your Preaching

    D.   The Attitude of Respect (Nehemiah 8:5)

    E.   The Attitude of Responding (Nehemiah 8:6; Hebrews 2:1; 3:7,15; 4:2)
          1.   Saying "amen"
          2.   Lifting up hands
          3.   Bowing their heads
          4.   Worshipping with face to the ground
          5.   Wept as a sign of brokenness

III. THE TEN WORST LISTENERS

    A.   Mr. Uninterested: seems bored, apathetic, in need of attitude adjustment

    B.   Mr. Detailer: overly impressed with minute details and misses the main point

    C.   Mr. Critical: criticizes the speaker's delivery, person, topic or any other handy target

    D.   Mr. Outliner: His only flexibility is with the color of pen he uses for notetaking. Everything must fit into his outline format.

    E.   Mr. Overstimulated: Each point sends this receiver tripping out on a private wave frequency.

    F.   Mr. Faker: Fakes attention and is overly passive. Has a dove attitude toward new information. Especially true in adults. Pseudo-politeness.

    G.   Mr. Distracter: Tolerates or creates distractions. Misses the message of the speaker and causes others to miss it also.

    H.   Mr. Wasteful: Wastes the time differential between speech speed and thought speed.

    I.   Mr. Lazy Mind: Cannot tolerate using the gray matter. Avoids listening to difficult material.

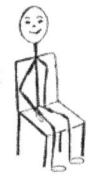

    J.   Mr. Biased: Emotion-laden words send him off on a private judgmental trip.

Empowering Your Preaching

Simple Steps in Evaluating Your Preaching

I. **EVALUATING THE STRUCTURE**

   A. Was it the mind of God, something you knew God wanted communicated?

   B. Was it well prepared?

   C. Was it biblical in aim and in content?

   D. Does your sermon have movement to it? A forward motion? A flow?

   E. Does your sermon have unity to it?

   F. Does your sermon have definite points and parts? Do you spend sufficient time on each part?

   G. Does your sermon have a clear, central point? Is it easy to remember? Is it stated clearly?

II. **EVALUATING THE MESSAGE**

   A. Is it interesting?

   B. Is it true?

   C. Is it biblical?

   D. Is it positive? Good news?

   E. Is it relevant to this audience (helpful, understandable)?

   F. Is there a call to some kind of action?

   G. Is it humorous?

   H. Are there good illustrations?

   I. Is it compassionate or judgmental?

   J. Is it logical? Is there an easily followed structure?

   K. Is it anchored in time and place?

   L. It is incarnational?

   M. Is it proclaiming or teaching?

Empowering Your Preaching

III. **EVALUATING THE MESSENGER**

    A. Does he have authority?

    B. Is he a real person (vulnerable, human)?

    C. Does he love the congregation or just love to preach?

    D. Is he a learner with the congregation or a remote teacher (pompous, pious)?

    E. What does his body language and face communicate (love, anger, joy, nervousness)?

    F. Does he have energy and excitement?

    G. Is he an original or a copy?

Voice Dynamics

I. **FIVE R'S FOR VOCAL DYNAMICS**
   (From International School of Christian Communicators, The Crystal Cathedral)

   A. Respiration: use abdominal breathing

   B. Recording: record your voice in a variety of settings and situations, record practice material

   C. Reciting: look for opportunities to read poems, scriptures, etc.; use the dramatic

   D. Reviewing: record samples and exercises – identify and eliminate trouble spots

   E. Resolving: to improve your voice, be consistent and use your new skills

II. **CHANGING THE WAY YOU USE YOUR VOICE**

   A. You are not changing your voice, but the way you use it.
      1. The changes in your voice will have people asking what is different. (You are in a good mood. What's different – your hair? Have you lost weight?)
      2. People will never say "I can see you are using your voice better."

   B. Changing requires practicing the 3 C's:
      1. Conscienceness
      2. Commitment
      3. Consistency

III. **MAINTAINING YOUR VOICE**

   A. Drink lots of water – 8 glasses a day.

   B. Avoid smoking or being in smoke-filled rooms.

   C. Avoid overuse or vocal abuse.

   D. Avoid harsh substances such as alcohol, ammonia and other chemicals.

   E. Avoid speaking over noise.

   F. Avoid straining your voice.

   G. Don't clear your throat. Cough instead.

   H. If your throat hurts or feels dry when you speak, don't ignore it. Something is wrong.

Empowering Your Preaching

IV. **SYMPTOMS OF PROBLEMS WITH YOUR VOICE**

    A. If any of these symptoms lasts for more than ten days, seek medical help.
1. Frequent bouts of hoarseness
2. Habitual throat clearing
3. Coughing
4. Vocal fatigue after speaking
5. Pain or irritation
6. Bulging veins in the neck
7. "Lump in the throat" feeling
8. Tightness in chest of neck
9. Tenderness in muscles in neck or shoulders
10. Too little or too much mucus
11. Pain in the base of the tongue
12. Reduced vocal range
13. Pitch breaks
14. Phonation breaks
15. Poor endurance
16. Raspy voice

    B. Signs of vocal abuse:
1. Nodules
2. Polyps

Empowering Your Preaching

A Pentecostal Approach to Scripture

How should Scripture be approached? On this question we believe Pentecostals have some insights which no else can offer. We Pentecostals bear distinctive witness to a reality and dimension of life in the Holy Spirit, out of which a uniquely Pentecostal approach to Scripture emerges. Some of the key aspects of this reality of life in the Spirit and their import for a Pentecostal approach to Scripture are described in the following:

1. *The Holy Spirit addresses us in ways which transcend human reason.* We see this especially in the gifts of the Spirit (I Corinthians 12;14) but also in more subtle ways (Romans 8:1-27). Thus we know that there is a vital place for emotion as well as reason, for imagination as well as logic, for mystery as well as certainty, and for that which is narrative and dramatic as well as that which is propositional and systematic. Consequently, we appreciate Scripture not just as an object which we interpret but as a living Word which interprets us and through which the Spirit flows in ways that we cannot dictate, calculate or program. This means that our Bible study must be open to surprises and even times of waiting or tarrying before the Lord.

2. *Experience is vital to know the truth.* Pentecostal faith is not, as some have caricatured, an experience-based faith. Yet we Pentecostals do see an inseparable interplay between knowledge and lived-experience, where knowing about God and directly experiencing God perpetually inform and depend upon one another. This accords with the biblical vs. the common secular understanding of knowledge. In the Old Testament this is seen in the very word for knowledge, yada, which points beyond the conceptualization of an object to the actualization of a relationship. This is why yada is used for marital lovemaking (e.g. Genesis 4:1) and covenantal intimacy (e.g. Jeremiah 1:5; 22:16; 31:34). This understanding of knowledge is carried forward into the New Testament, so that, as I John teaches, "he who does not love does not know God" (4:8). We Pentecostals have appreciated this biblical emphasis upon lived-experience by including testimony in our times of gathering around the Word and by expecting not just information but transformation. What would Pentecostal preaching be without the altar call? And by the same token, what would Pentecostal Bible study be without explicit recognition and overt responding to the transforming call of God's Word? Can our approach to Bible study be Pentecostal if the question "What then shall we do?" is left unexpressed and unanswered or otherwise loses that urgency which marks a people of last-days expectancy and global mission?

3. *The Spirit calls every individual believer to be a witness of the truth* (cf. Acts 1:8). The priesthood (I Peter 2:5,9) and prophethood (Numbers 11:27-29; Joel 2:28-32; Acts 2:16-20) of all believers has distinct reality among Pentecostals in our experience of the Spirit being "poured out upon all flesh" (Acts 2:17). The Spirit gives to some the special gift of teaching but calls every believer to walk in the light for themselves (I John 1:7; 2:27; cf. Ephesians 4:7-17) and to be a Christ-like witness of that light before others (I John 4:13-17; Matthew 5:14). These concerns claim deep roots in our Pentecostal heritage. We see them in the enduring adage, "one should walk in the light as it shines upon his/her path" (the tradition underlying the Lighted Pathway), and in our expectation that every convert should be a first-hand partaker and bearer of the Word, thereby edifying the congregation and evangelizing the lost.

4. ***Knowledge of the truth is inseparable from active membership in the localized body of Christ.*** The corporate experience of the faith has been especially vital to us Pentecostals. Pentecostal faith is born out of a gathering together of believers (Acts 2:1-4) and continues to be nurtured and sustained by this same communion of the saints (Acts 2:42-47). We have long testified to the special revelation of Christ "where two or three are gathered together" in His name (Matthew 18:20). We have decried "forsaking the assembling of ourselves together," for here we experience the indispensable ministry of "exhorting one another, and so much the more, as we see the day approaching" (Hebrews 10:25). In other words, here we experience the reality of being the body of Christ, bound together as a particular historical community with holy bonds of mutual interdependence and accountability. Here the Holy Spirit speaks as nowhere else, bestowing and blending gifts among all the members in order to make manifest God's Word in the edification of the whole body (I Corinthians 12;14; Ephesians 4; Romans 12). The first general assembly of the Church of God in 1906 grew directly out of this conviction, with explicit appeal to the Jerusalem Council of Acts 15, and this same commitment to gathering around the Word in the Spirit remains a mark of truly Pentecostal gatherings to this day.

Ironically, while certain cutting-edge trends in recent theology have moved closer to these Pentecostal emphases (e.g., narrative theology, theology as praxis, the community's role in interpretation, etc.) we Pentecostals have tended to move further away from these emphases as we have adopted the approaches, methods, and, in some cases, the curricula of other (non-Pentecostal) traditions. We believe that the Pentecostal content which we have been attempting to infuse secondarily into our Bible study is being effectively sabotaged by the powerful and persuasive teaching impact of non-Pentecostal methods. We consider the pursuit of a distinctly Pentecostal approach to Scripture to be absolutely essential right now if we are to survive and our children are to become Pentecostal. We submit that there is a crying need and a divine mandate before us right now to recover an approach to Scripture which will "quench not the Spirit!" (I Thessalonians 5:19).

So, What's Cooking?

Behold, a cook went forth to cook. And as he cooked, his household was nourished and satisfied, so much so that they went out into the highways and hedges and brought in the hungry and thirsty, and the house was filled.

But it came to pass one day that the cook discovered a cookbook. In this cookbook were recipes and menus, and also analytical charts explaining the nutrition in various foods. There were also beautiful pictures of succulent dishes.

"I will now step aside and examine this great book," said the cook. "It must have great value, for it was published by a cooking school that trained the three greatest cooks in the land."

So, he read in the book day by day, while feeding his household leftovers. He became so excited about the menus, charts, and pictures, that he wanted to share them with his household.

"My household is too large for all of them to see this book," he said to himself. "What shall I do? I know what I shall do! I shall purchase an overhead projector and thus enable everyone to benefit from the wealth of material in this cookbook."

So, he purchased a projector and began at each meal to explain where food came from, what it contains, and how it can be prepared. His household became engrossed in the charts and pictures. Before long, they began to bring notebooks and pencils to the table instead of knives and forks. But by then, all the leftovers were gone and the cook had not prepared any new meals. The household spent their time doing nothing but discussing some new menu or analytical chart.

And it came to pass that the household started to become weak and grow thin. Yea, the cook himself began to lose weight so that he could no longer carry his overhead projector to the dining room. "I will make myself a dish such as I used to make," he said to himself. And he did. As the aroma of the meal wafted through the house, the family gathered at the table as before, but this time they came with their knives and forks. Soon it was like old times again, as they ate and were nourished. The cook had great joy as he saw the family gain weight and grow in strength.

And he said to himself, "Yea, this may be a fine book, but it is not substitute for a good meal. My household cannot thrive on menus, recipes, pictures, and the chemical analyses of the food. I will arise and go to the kitchen and spend my time preparing dishes that will feed my family."

And he did; and the cookbook gathered dust on the shelf, while in the bookstores, it was selling like hotcakes.

Eutychus X

Warren Wiersbe and David Wiersbe. <u>The Elements of Preaching</u>. (Wheaton, IL: Tyndale House Publishers, 1986), pp. 107-109.

Preacher's Basic Research Library

Greek Research Tools
1. New Strong's Exhaustive Concordance by James Strong (Thomas Nelson/Word, 2000)
2. The New Englishman's Greek Concordance by George V. Wigram (Hendrickson Publishers, 1996)
3. The New Greek English Lexicon of the New Testament by Joseph Thayer (Hendrickson Publishers, 1996)
4. New International Dictionary of New Testament Theology, 4 volumes by Colin Brown (Zondervan, 1986)
5. Word Pictures in the New Testament by A.T. Robertson (Broadman/Holman)
6. The Word Study New Testament and Concordance, 2 volumes by Ralph Winter (Tyndale House, 1978)
7. Vincent's New Testament Word Studies, 4 volumes by Marvin Vincent (Hendrickson Publishers, 1986)
8. Word Meanings in the New Testament by Ralph Earle (Hendrickson Publishers, 1986)
9. New Testament Words by William Barclay (Westminster/John Knox, 1974)
10. Theological Dictionary of the New Testament by Gerhard Kittel (Eerdmans Publishing, 1964 for the 10 volume set or 1985 for one volume set)
11. Vine's Complete Expository Dictionary of Old and New Testament Words by W.E. Vine (Thomas Nelson/Word, 1985)

Hebrew Research Tools
1. The Englishman's Hebrew Concordance of the Old Testament by George V. Wigram (Hendrickson Publishers, 1996)
2. Gesenius' Hebrew-Chaldee Lexicon to the Old Testament by H.W.F. Gesenius (Baker/Revell, 1979)
3. Theological Wordbook of the Old Testament, 2 volumes edited by R.L. Harris, G.L. Archer, Jr. and B.K. Waltke (Moody Press, 1980)
4. Wilson's Old Testament Word Studies by William Wilson (Hendrickson Publishers)

Commentaries
1. Lenski New Testament Commentaries, 12 volumes by R.C.H. Lenski (Hendrickson Publishers, 1942)
2. Barnes Notes on the Old and New Testaments by Albert Barnes (Baker/Revell)
3. Explore the Book by J. Sidlow Baxter (Zondervan Publishing)
4. Keil & Delitzsch Old Testament Commentary on the Old Testament, 10 volumes by C.F. Keil (Hendrickson Publishers, 2001)
5. Expostions of the Holy Scriptures by MacLaren (Baker Publishing), 17 volumes.
6. The Preacher's Homiletic Commentary, 31 volumes (Baker Publishing)

Empowering Your Preaching

Limited Bibliography on Preaching

Author	Title	Publisher	Year
Adams, Jay E.	Pulpit Speech	Presbyterian and Reformed	1971
Adams, Jay E.	Preaching With Purpose	Zondervan	1982
Adams, Jay E.	Preaching to the Heart	Presbyterian and Reformed	1983
Blackwood, Andrew	The Fine Art of Preaching	Baker	1976
Bounds, E.M.	Preacher and Prayer	The Christian Witness	1907
Broadus, John A.	Preparation and Delivery of Sermons	A.C. Armstrong and Sons	1898
Brooks, Phillips	Lectures on Preaching	E.P. Dutton and Company	1907
Brown, Dean Charles R.	The Art of Preaching	MacMillan Company	1922
Brown, Elijah P.	The Point and Purpose of Preaching	Fleming H. Revell	1917
Buttrick, George A.	Jesus Came Preaching	Charles Scribner and Sons	1931
Clowney, Edmund P.	Preaching and Biblical Theology	Presbyterian and Reformed	1973
Dodd, C.H.	The Apostolic Preaching and Its Developments	Harper and Row	1964
Evans, William	How to Prepare Sermons	Moody Press	1964
Hybells, Bill; Briscoe, Stuart; and Robinson, Haddon	Mastering Contemporary Preaching	Multnomah Press	1990
Jones, D. Martyn Lloyd	Preaching and Preachers	Zondervan	1971
Kennedy, Gerald	His Word Through Preaching	Harper and Brothers	1947
Ker, John	The History of Preaching	Hodder and Stoughton	1869
Kinlaw, Dennis	Preaching in the Spirit	Asbury Press	1978
Lewis, Ralph L.	Inductive Preaching	Abingdon Press	1957
MacLaod, Donald	The Problem of Preaching	Fortress Press	1987
Morgan, G. Campbell	Preaching	Fleming H. Revel	
Moule, H.C.G.	To My Younger Brethren	Hodder and Stoughton	1892
Nee, Watchman	Ministry of God	Christian Fellowship Publishers	1971
Spurgeon, C.H.	Lectures to My Students	Passmore and Alabaster	1897
Stott, John R.W.	Between Two Worlds	William B. Eerdmans	1982
Wiersbe, Warren	The Wycliffe Handbook of Preaching and Preachers	Moody Press	1984

Sermons, Resources and PowerPoints

This next section contains twelve sermons that Pastor Frank has preached at City Bible Church over the last several years. Most of these sermons are the first in a series. For further information on the material presented in the sermon, you can purchase the tape series or the book.

Sermon Title	Tape Series	Book	Preaching Method
Believer and Spiritual Warfare	Maximizing Your Warfare Potential (8 tapes)	Maximizing Your Warfare Potential Syllabus	Doctrinal
Building Gate Churches for the 21st Century	The Gate Church Tape Series (2 tapes)	The Gate Church	Inspirational
Call to Be Equipped	The Biblical Responsibility of Every Believer (7 tapes)		Practical
Call to Cell Commitment	The Biblical Responsibility of Every Believer (7 tapes)		Practical
Kingdom Priorities: Jesus' Laws of Living	Kingdom Priorities (8 tapes)		Expositional
Kingdom Priorities: Renewing Kingdom Lifestyle	Kingdom Priorities (8 tapes)		Expositional
Preparation and Hindrances to Prayer	Seven Power Points of Prayer (10 tapes)	Seasons of Intercession Seasons of Revival	Expositional
Renewed Relationship	Rewards of a Renewed Soul (8 tapes)		Expositional
Responding to the Call to Become a Church of Intercession	Gap Standing and Hedge Building (12 tapes)	Seasons of Intercession	Expositional
The Unsearchable Riches of Christ's Mercy	The Unsearchable Riches of Christ (2 tapes)		Thematic
We Can Touch the World	We Can Touch the World (1 tape)		Expositional
Weaving Through Building Relationships	Net Power & Principle (8 tapes)		Expositional

To purchase the listed products:
- Shop online at www.citychristianpublishing.com.
- Call City Christian Publishing at 1-800-777-6057.
- Email City Christian Publishing at order@citychristianpublishing.com.

The Believer and Spiritual Warfare

Isaiah 42:13; Isaiah 54:17 — Pastor Frank Damazio

Our Enemies:
- The world: system, spirit
- The flesh: appetites not under control
- The devil: evil spirit

I Peter 5:8-9; I John 3:8; Isaiah 42:13; 54:17; Matthew 11:12; Revelation 12:11; I John 4:4; Ephesians 6:10-17

INTRODUCTION: In spiritual warfare one must never underestimate or over-estimate the strength of the enemy. The Lord is with His army and will not fail us. We fight in His name and power, whereas our enemies fight in their own power. We fight with enemies that have been spoiled, whose weapons are blunted, whose power is limited. We know from Scripture that spiritual warfare is a fact. We will fight. We will encounter real satanic opposition. We also know from Scripture that we will win if we follow the biblical guidelines for winning spiritual battles. Satan reigns over an aerial kingdom of hierarchies and spiritual powers, a kingdom on earth in the world of men. He governs by means of an organized spiritual evil network.

I. STRUGGLE AGAINST ORGANIZED SPIRITUAL NETWORKS

Ephesians 6:10,12-13 "In conclusion, be strong in the Lord — be empowered through your union with Him; draw your strength from Him — that strength which His [boundless] might provides. For we are not wrestling with flesh and blood — contending only with physical opponents — but against the despotisms, against the powers, against [the master spirits who are] the world rulers of this present darkness, against the spirit forces of wickedness in the heavenly (supernatural) sphere. Therefore put on God's complete armor, that you may be able to resist and stand your ground on the evil day [of danger], and having done all [the crisis demands], to stand [firmly in your place]." (Amplified)

- Worldview: This is one's basic assumptions about reality. It has to do with one's personal or a group's collective view of reality. There are two realities: There is reality as God has made and sees it. There is reality as we finite and imperfect human beings perceive it. Usually we see the world, both physical and other aspects of it, as we have been taught to see it. It is part of our world view to assume that our way of seeing the world is right. We Westerns have been taught, or allowed to assume, that our perception of reality is right. We must have a biblical worldview.

Empowering Your Preaching

- Biblical worldview = the invisible world of angels, spirits, demons and God exists. There is a war between God's kingdom and Satan's. We live in the presence of evil powers that seek to destroy our life in any way possible. There is no truce, no hiding, no retreating. No giving up or giving over any ground. Folks, we are at war!
- Bernie May, director of Wycliffe Bible Translators: "I need to learn as much as possible about spirit warfare. Our struggle out there is not against the climate, the malaria or the false religions. Our struggle is against the principalities and powers, against the world rulers of this present darkness, against the spiritual hosts of wickedness in heavenly places."

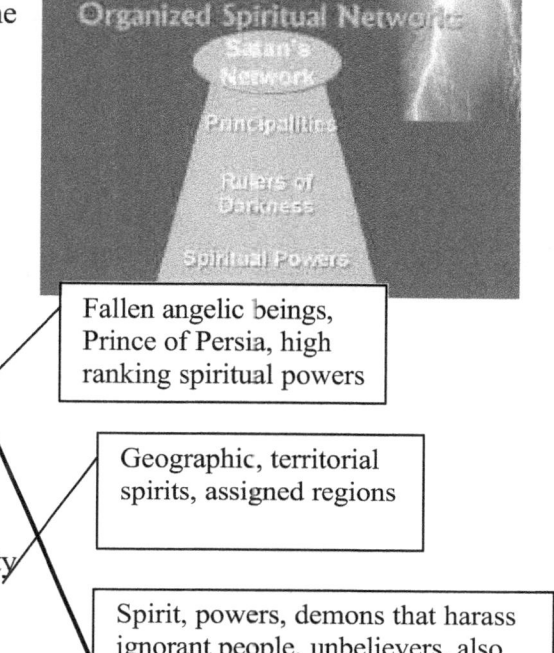

God of this age
Prince and power of the air
Ruler of this world
Whole world under his influence

SATAN'S NETWORK
II Cor 4:4; Eph 2:2; Jn 12:31; I Jn 5:19

Principalities
Leaders of an order or rank

Fallen angelic beings, Prince of Persia, high ranking spiritual powers

Rulers of Darkness
Governors in seats of authority

Geographic, territorial spirits, assigned regions

Spiritual Powers
Demonic spirits attacking continually

Spirit, powers, demons that harass ignorant people, unbelievers, also unprepared believers

2 Cor 4:4; Eph 2:2; John 12:31; I Jn 5:19
Not to be born of God is to be wholly under the power of the evil one.

II. SATAN IS STRATEGIZING YOUR DEFEAT AND DESTRUCTION

- *I Peter 5:8-9 "Be well-balanced - temperate, sober-minded; be vigilant and cautious at all times. For that enemy of yours, the devil, roams around like a lion roaring in fierce hunger, seeking someone to seize upon and devour. Withstand him.*
- *Be firm in faith against his onset, rooted, established, strong, immovable and steadfast." (Amplified)*
  John 10:10 *The thief does not come except to steal, and to kill, and to destroy.*

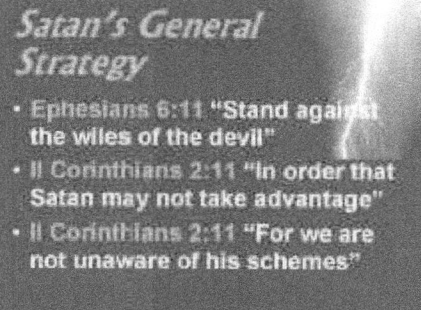

A. Satan's General Strategy

 1. Ephesians 6:11 "Stand against the wiles of the devil"
    - Wiles (Gr *methodia*): to follow up and investigate by methods and a settled plan, to plan crafty tricks, schemes.

 2. II Corinthians 2:11 "...in order that Satan might not take advantage"
    - Advantage (Gr *pleonekteo*): wanting more, to take the greater part, to plunder

 3. II Corinthians 2:11 "...for we are not unaware of his schemes"
    - Schemes (Gr *noema*): to have a definite thought against, to ponder at length, to plan very meticulously, to strategize

B. Satan's Specific Strategy

 1. Quickly snatching away the spiritual seeds sown into our hearts through preaching, prayer, and rhema quickened words before the seed can take root. (Mt 13:19)

 2. Quietly and persistently taking away your spiritual rights and the spiritual ground God has given you, setting up his ownership little by little (Eph 4:7; II Samuel 23:11-12)

    - II Samuel 23:11-12 The Philistines came to take Shammah's hill that was full of lentils. The rest of the people fled, but he took his stand in the middle of the plot of ground and defended it, striking the Philistines until he brought about a great victory!

 3. Repeatedly using the art of condemnation to shake our assurance, cripple our confidence and devastate our future hopes and dreams. (Rev 12:9-11)

 4. Overwhelm our soul by a chain of unusual bad experiences, irritations, small calamities so that he may destroy our faith and gain control over us through fear. (Mt 17:15; Acts 10:38; II Corinthians 12:7; Isaiah 59:19)

 5. To hinder the church from moving into spiritual blessings by attacking key leaders or key people, creating a spirit of negativism, magnifying little problems, relational conflicts, spiritual unrest, murmuring, anyway or anything to cause division to as to stop spiritual momentum. (Isaiah 57:14; 62:10)

6. To attack believers through spiritual parasites that attach themselves to our spiritual life, draining our strength and virtues over an extended period of time. They attack to our mind and emotions.
- Parasite: one who derives advantage or sustenance from another and gives nothing in return. Attaches itself to the system, draining off life, health and energy.
- Leech: one who clings closely to another and extracts whatever he can for his own advantage.
- Psalm 23: Anoint my head with oil. The oil was medicinal to protect from the ticks, parasites and leeches.

C. Satan's Seasonal Strategy
*Luke 4:13 "When the devil had finished all this tempting, he left Him **until a more opportune time.**"*
1. Satanic attacks in seasons of <u>fruitfulness</u> (Genesis 49:22-26)
2. Satanic attacks in seasons of <u>sacrifice</u> (Genesis 15:1-11; Matthew 13:4)
3. Satanic attacks in seasons of <u>breakthrough</u> (Exodus 14:15-16; I Corinthians 16:9)
4. Satanic attacks in seasons of <u>intense prayer intercession</u> (Daniel 9:3-4; 10:12-14)

III. SPIRITUAL WARFARE 101 WEAPONS

A. The Weapon of <u>Spiritual Knowledge and Insights</u> Concerning Satan's Ways
II Corinthians 2:11

B. The Weapon of <u>Spiritual Strength and Security</u> from Christ's Work on the Cross
Revelation 12:11; I John 3:8; Colossians 2:15

C. The Weapon of <u>Spiritual Placement and Commitment</u> to My Church, My Spiritual Family
Ephesians 4:16; Proverbs 27:8; I Cor 12:18,28

D. The Weapon of <u>Personal Prayer and Corporate Prayer</u> for Renewing and Refocusing
Ephesians 6:18; Deuteronomy 32:30; Acts 1:14

E. The Weapon of <u>Using God's Word</u> for Defeating the Devil
- *I John 4:4 You are of God, little children, and have overcome them, because He who is in you is greater than he who is in the world.*

- *Romans 8:37 Yet in all these things we are more than conquerors through Him who loved us.*
- *II Corinthians 10:3-4 For though we walk in the flesh, we do not war according to the flesh. For the weapons of our warfare are not carnal but mighty in God for pulling down strongholds.*
- *Isaiah 54:17 No weapon formed against you shall prosper, and every tongue which rises against you in judgment you shall condemn. This is the heritage of the servants of the LORD, and their righteousness is from Me, says the LORD.*
- *Jude 1:9 Yet Michael the archangel, in contending with the devil, when he disputed about the body of Moses, dared not bring against him a reviling accusation, but said, "The Lord rebuke you!"*
- *Deuteronomy 28:7 The LORD will cause your enemies who rise against you to be defeated before your face; they shall come out against you one way and flee before you seven ways.*
- *Psalm 34:7 The angel of the LORD encamps all around those who fear Him, and delivers them.*
- *Revelation 12:11 And they overcame him by the blood of the Lamb and by the word of their testimony, and they did not love their lives to the death.*
- *James 4:7-8 Therefore submit to God. Resist the devil and he will flee from you. Draw near to God and He will draw near to you. Cleanse your hands, you sinners; and purify your hearts, you double-minded.*

F. The Weapon of Wearing the Full Armor of God
Ephesians 6:10-17

1. The Belt of Truth
2. The Breastplate of Righteousness
3. The Shoes of Peace
4. The Shield of Faith
5. The Helmet of Salvation
6. The Sword of the Spirit
7. The Prayer of Warfare

Empowering Your Preaching
Building Gate-Churches for the 21st Century

Pastor Frank Damazio

The gateway into a new millennium is upon us. We are about to enter into a new era, a new millennium, a new world. The gate of entry is open but many face it with feelings of anxiety, anticipation, or discouragement. The challenge before us is to establish powerful churches worldwide that bridge this gateway. I call them "Gate-Churches".

"America is at a turning point in its history," George Barna informs us in his book *The Second Coming of the Church:* The decisions we make in the next few years regarding who we are and the values we stand for will seal the moral and spiritual fate of America for decades to come. The decadence and darkness of our nation are more profound than since the founding of this nation more than two centuries ago. The only power that can cleanse and restore this nation is the power of Christ. And the primary way in which that power is manifested is by Christ's followers serving God and humanity by being the Church—that is, the true representative of Jesus Christ.

This is our time of testing. We must prove that we are what we claim to be, or we will certainly lose the platform to influence the world for Christ. That privileged position is already slipping from our grasp. Given the moral and spiritual demise of our culture, maintaining that position is not an insignificant challenge. And the sad truth is that the Christian church, as we now know it, is not geared up to meet that challenge.

Our situation is not hopeless, but it is urgent. Time is of the essence. Godly, strategic leadership, dedicated to the fulfillment of God's vision for America and His church, is demanded." (Thomas Trask, <u>The Choice</u>. Zondervan Publishing, page 165)

"Billy Graham sites four challenges we will face as we communicate the gospel in the new millennium.
1. Excessive Urbanization: This means that poverty-stricken multitudes of the world's 6 billion people (50 percent who are under age twenty-five) will be living in large cities.
2. Secularism will continue to supplant Christianity in former strongholds, especially in Europe, communicating a message that excludes God and moral and spiritual absolutes.
3. Non-Christian religions are burgeoning where secularism isn't, with cults and non-Western religions proliferating in the United States and worldwide.
4. Political changes can mean either open or increasingly aggressive closed doors to Christianity in the Middle East, Asia, Eastern Europe, and Russia, where the prayer and partnership of Christian remnants are especially important."[1]

Empowering Your Preaching

I. **THE MAKING OF A GATE-CHURCH PASTOR/LEADER**
   Genesis 27-28

   A. The Journey of Destiny – *From Beersheba to Haran*
      Genesis 28:10; 26:33
      - Beersheba: Well of oath
      - Haran: parched land

      The contexts of Jacob's circumstances plays into the contexts of God sovereignly visiting him.

      The Journey of Destiny
      1. An emotional **stressful circumstance** which becomes surprisingly complicated
      2. A **character flaw** resulting in a failure-mistake
      3. A severely **damaged relationship**
      4. An upheaval of **life's comfort zones** and routines

      1. An emotional <u>stressful circumstance</u> which becomes surprisingly complicated (Genesis 27:1-19)
         - He had just gone through a lifetime of emotional stress and is now in the presence of his dying father.

      2. A <u>character flaw</u> resulting in a failure-mistake (Genesis 27:35)
         - He has just committed a character sin of deception, lying, stealing a birthright, failure.

      3. A severely <u>damaged relationship</u> (Genesis 27:41-42)
         - He has caused his brother to hate him and seek to kill him. A relationship has been severely damaged.

      4. An upheaval of <u>life's comfort zones</u> and routines (Genesis 27:43)
         - He is now fleeing for his life. Uprooted from his family, friends and city, he is fleeing to another place.

   B. The Hidden Sovereignty of God
      - "To understand the sovereignty of God is to realize that God is God and that he can do anything he desires, whenever he wishes, to whomever he wants. To me this means that because I love the Lord with all of my heart, he will lead me to do his will, place me in any geographical location, or give me any responsibility that he wishes. He will also determine what is best for me as I grow more Christlike."[2]

      The Hidden Sovereignty of God
      1. A certain place
      2. An ordinary stone
      3. A surprise dream
      4. A sovereign place

      1. A <u>certain place</u>
         Genesis 28:11 "...so he came to a certain place"
         - Sixty miles from Beersheba, situated in the mountains of Ephraim, about three hours north of Jerusalem, several days journey.
         - He had no idea that this accidental place was a certain place: a no big deal place, a nothing special or prophetic place, a place to rest and sleep, no expectations.

2. An <u>ordinary stone</u>
   Genesis 28:11 "...and he took one of the stones"
   - History: the track of pilgrims winds through the uneven valley covered, as with gravestones, large sheets of bare rocks, some few here and there standing up like the monuments of death to vision, courage or risks.
   - He had no idea the stone he chose accidentally (with no careful selection, just another ordinary stone) was more than just a pillar or a stone to use for menial tasks.

3. A <u>surprise dream</u>
   Genesis 28:12 "...then he dreamed"
   - He didn't expect a dream at this certain place, this normal, every-day regular place. He didn't expect a visitation personally. He was not in a visitation mode, not in a God-encountering mode.

4. A <u>sovereign place</u>
   Genesis 28:16 "...Jacob awoke... The Lord is in this place and I did not know it"
   Genesis 28:17 "...how awesome is this place!"

II. THE MAKING OF A GATE-CHURCH VISION
Genesis 28:17 "This is none other than the house of God. This is the gate of heaven."
Genesis 28:19 "And he called the name of that place Bethel"

A. A Gate-Church in Every Place
   Gate-churches are called to establish open heavens in the city, thus changing the atmosphere in the city and the region. These gate-churches are apostolic in calling and apostolic in their leadership. A gate-church doesn't think for itself only but for the city and for all the churches in the region. A gate-church opens up new territory, new truths, and new power. It forges the way for others to receive.

   The Making of a Gate-Church Vision
   Gate-churches are called to establish open heavens in the city, thus changing the atmosphere in the city and region. These gate-churches are apostolic in calling and apostolic in their leadership. A gate-church does not think for itself only but for the city and for all the churches in the region. A gate-church opens up new territory, new truths and new power. It forges the way for others to receive.

   1. Gate Linguistically
      a. Hebrew: A structure closing or enclosing a large opening through a wall or a barrier through which people and things pass to another area, a new area.
      b. Dictionary: A way into something, a passageway or a channel; signifies both the opening and the passage; an avenue, an opening, a way.

Empowering Your Preaching

2. Gate Symbolically
   The gates of Old Testament cities became symbolic. There are basically four applications suggested by the role of city gates during Old Testament times.
   a. A place that controlled access and provided strongly fortified protection.
   b. A place where legal or governmental leaders of the city sat at the gates and handed down judicial decisions. (Deut 25:7)
   c. A place where business and social functions occurred, where business contracts were made and witnessed. (Ruth 4:1,11)
   d. A place where prophetic messages were brought to the city. (Jer 17:19; 7:2)

B. Characteristics of the Gate-Church

   1. *The spiritual atmosphere of the Gate-church*
      God's glory permeates the atmosphere of the Gate-church. There is a spirit of unity that is manifested in joy and peace because problems are safely confronted, dealt with and forgiven. (Gen 28:12; II Chronicles 31:2; Psalm 24:7)

   2. *The Gate-Church prayer intercession ladder*
      God has mandated that His house be called a "house of prayer" (Isaiah. 56:7). Gate-Church leaders, therefore, take responsibility for establishing a ladder of prayer intercession where God's people can express their hearts to God and clearly hear His voice. (Gen 28:12)
      a. Interceding leaders
      b. Interceding people
      c. Interceding atmosphere
      d. Interceding churches
      e. Interceding principles
      f. Interceding for cities and nations

Empowering Your Preaching

3. *The Gate-Church implements present prophetic truths.*
   The same wind that brings refreshing can also bring destruction. The fire we use to warm ourselves, if out of control, brings devastation. The Gate-Church leader must learn how to approach new truths and prophetic trends for today with wisdom, balance and patience. (Gen 28:13,15; Is 62:10)

   > **Twelve Characteristics of the Gate-Church**
   > 4. The Gate-Church grows in quantity and quality (Gen 28:13-14)
   > 5. The Gate-Church blesses and builds families (Gen 28:14)
   > 6. The Gate-Church door of divine opportunity (Gen 28:15)

4. *The Gate Church Grows in Quantity and Quality*
   Gate Churches are made up of fishers of men and women whose nets are knotted together with agape love and covenantal relationships. These relational ties form a safety net that is strong enough to hold the quantity needed for the endtimes catch. (Gen 28:13-14)

5. *The Gate Church Blesses and Builds Families*
   The Gate Church must not only concentrate on saving the lost outside the church, but it should also focus on preserving the fruit from the biological reproduction that has been placed by God in the church. (Gen 28:14)

6. *The Gate-Church Door of Divine Opportunity*
   God is the one who opens our doors of opportunity. He holds those doors open until we are ready to enter. Therefore, we do not have to fear that our adversaries, our inadequacies or our obstacles can shut what God has opened for us. (Gen 28:15)

   > **Twelve Characteristics of the Gate-Church**
   > 7. The Gate-Church has awesome worship (Gen 28:16-17; II Chron 5:11-14; Is 60:18; Ps 24:7)
   > 8. The Gate-Church builds with stones and pillars (II Chron 2:1-10; Gen 28:18-19; I Kings 5:17-18)
   > 9. The Gate-Church is a word-driven church (Gen 28:19)

7. *The Gate Church Has Awesome Worship*
   Worship in the Gate Church is not about performing to seek the applause of people; it is physically and spiritually preparing and yielding ourselves to the King of kings so that His presence can be experienced by one and all. (Genesis 28:16-17; II Chronicles 5:11-14; Isaiah 60:18; Psalm 24:7)

8. *The Gate Church Builds with Stones and Pillars*
   The Lord uses living stones to build a Gate Church. These are people who know where they fit and are willing to function there faithfully. God sends pillars to support leaders in the Gate Church; people who are unmoved by circumstances and willing to endure through crises and pressures. (II Chronicles 2:1-10; Genesis 28:18-19; I Kings 5:17-18; I Peter 2:5)

Empowering Your Preaching

9. *The Gate Church is a word-driven church*
   We know Christ through the Bible, and we understand the Bible through the knowledge of Christ. Therefore, the Gate Church is a word-preaching and word-teaching church. (Gen 28:19)

10. *The Gate Church Is a Giving Church*
    The Gate Church believes that the giving of the tithe is only the beginning of giving, only the foundation for more generous acts of faith and sacrifice. (Gen 28:20-22; Isaiah 60:11)

11. *The Gate Church Opens the Gate of Healing and Miracles*
    The Great Commission to the church, includes healing the sick. The Gate Church believes that the balanced ministry of the church is teaching, preaching and healing. We are to make people whole in body, soul and spirit, by believing in the invisible, the unexplainable, and doing the impossible. (Gen 28:12; Jn 1:50-51; Jn 5:2)

III. THE GATES THAT THE GATEKEEPER GUARDS

A. Gatekeepers in Every Place for Every Gate (I Chronicles 9:18; II Chr 8:14; 35:15)

B. Ten Gates to Continually Guard and Keep Open

1. Gatekeeper of the Vision Gate (Prov 29:18)
   - Pastoring the vision, the dream given to you.

2. Gatekeeper of the Harvest Gate (Neh 3:3)
   - The spirit of evangelism

3. Gatekeeper of the Values Gate (Neh 3:6)
   - Keep the basics as priority. Build on foundation truths. Know how to establish and strengthen these truths continually.

4. Gatekeeper of the River Gate (Fountain) (Nehemiah 3:15)
   - Pastoring the Holy Spirit activity, flow, river, pastoring the subjective.

5. Gatekeeper of the City Gate (Nehemiah 2:13; II Chronicles 35:15)
   - Relationship to the city, city itself, city leaders, city atmosphere.

Empowering Your Preaching

6. Gatekeeper of the Prayer and Praise Gate (Psalm 47:7; 111:1; I Peter 2:5)
   - Pastoring the worship department.

7. Gatekeeper of the Warfare Gate (Genesis 49:23; 22:17; 32:10; 32:18; I Kings 11:5-11)
   - Keeping watch over the important issues and people.

8. Gatekeeper of the Miracle Gate (Acts 3:10; 10:17)

9. Gatekeeper of the Finance Gate (II Chronicles 31:14)

10. Gatekeeper of the Glory of God Gate (Ezekiel 43:4; 44:4)

---

[1] Thomas E. Trask and Wayde I. Goodall. The Choice: Embracing God's Vision in the New Millennium. Grand Rapids: Zondervan Publishing, 1999. Page 20.
[2] Ibid. Page 45.

Empowering Your Preaching

A Call to Be Equipped
The Biblical Responsibility of Every Believer

Pastor Frank Damazio

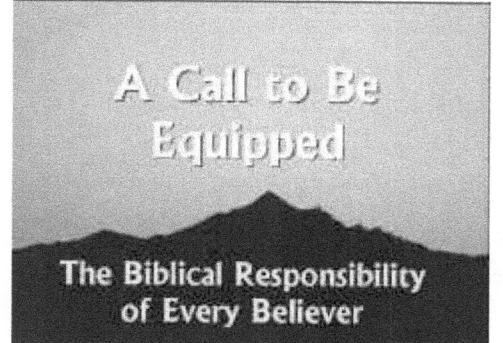

INTRODUCTION: Every believer has a destiny to fulfill in God. This destiny involves finding their spiritual gifting. Every believer must dedicate themselves to this destiny, God's purpose for their life. The early church was organized in a way that let all members of each congregation play an active role in the church's life. Within her membership, the early church had a variety of people with different spiritual gifts that were profitable to the entire local body of believers. The two main areas of gift-function were those Christians who guided and labored in the Word of God, and those who participated in the various congregational ministries of I Corinthians 12:4-11 and Romans 12:3-8. These portions of scripture enumerated the various congregational ministries in the church. Though these verses do not provide the complete list of ministries, they give us a good idea of the diversity of the gifted congregational ministries: the word of wisdom, the word of knowledge, the gift of faith, gifts of healing, the working of miracles, prophecy, the discernment of spirits, various kinds of tongues, the interpretation of tongues, serving, teaching, exhorting, giving, governing, showing mercy.

- *Larry Bird*: "To me," says basketball star Larry Bird, "a winner is someone who recognizes his God-given talents, works his tail off to develop them into skills, and uses those skills to accomplish his goals. Even when I lost, I learned what my weaknesses were, and I went out the next day to turn those weaknesses into strengths."
- *Martin Luther King*: "Everybody can be great because everybody can serve. You don't have to have a college degree to serve. You don't have to make your subject and verb agree to serve. You don't have to know about Plato and Aristotle, …Einstein's theory of relativity or the second theory of thermodynamics in physics to serve. You only need a heart full of grace and a soul generated by love."

I. SAVING GRACE AND EQUIPPING GRACE (Ephesians 4:7)

A. Saving Grace (Ephesians 2:5-8)
- *Chariti*: Saving grace refers to undeserved favor and is a constant reminder that God does not manifest acts of mercy toward people because they deserve them. Believers are trophies of God's grace to be displayed for eternity.

B. Equipping Grace (Ephesians 4:7)
1. Within the body of Christ each member enjoys a share of God's grace. This equipping grace denotes the grace provided for and manifested in the gift. The distribution of grace and so the distribution of grace-gifts is in Christ's hands and apportioned as he decides.

Empowering Your Preaching

2. This grace endowment bestowed on "each <u>one</u> of us" implies that the recipient shall indeed recognize it as a gift and not as the product of his own skill or ingenuity. It is only one gift within the whole body, a measured or limited gift that also needs all the other gifted people.
3. Equipping grace results in Ephesians 4:16 which describes a coordinated body with each member fulfilling its member function by grace.

II. THE EQUIPPING OF ALL BELIEVERS

- Ephesians 4:11 lists the governmental ministries of the Body of Christ: apostle, prophet, evangelist, pastor and teacher. In the past, many Christians have viewed these gifted ministries as the only people in the church who have a specific work to do for the Lord. The governmental ministries oversee and develop these ministries in the rest of the Body of Christ. Ephesians 4:12 tells us that these five governmental ministries prepare the saints for their various ministries—but do NOT do all the ministering for the saints.

A. Ephesians 4:11-13

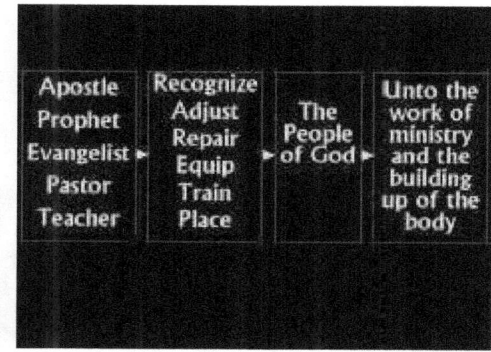

B. Ephesians 4:12 Diagram

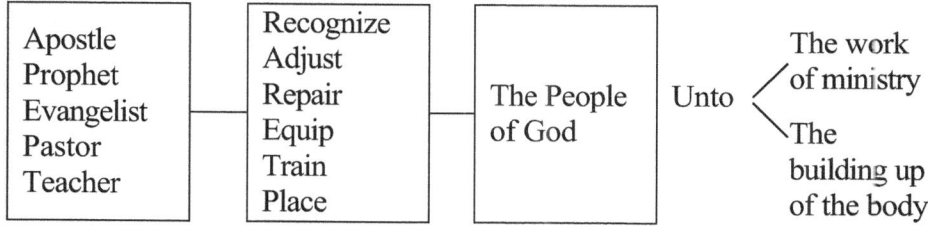

C. Defining the Word "Equip"

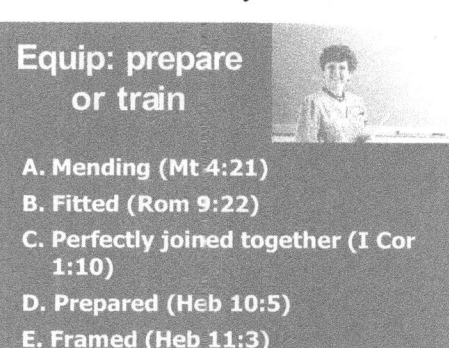

1. Greek - [*Katartismos*] - Preparing or training, to complete thoroughly, to repair, to adjust, a craftsman.

Empowering Your Preaching

2. *Katartismos* translated:

   a. **Mending**: James and John were bringing the broken strands of their nets together with the other strands so as to make their net function properly. They were mending, adjusting and equipping the <u>net</u> to do the work of fishing. Those strands that had been broken under the pressure of their work had to be mended. What they were doing in the natural was prophetic of what they were destined to do in the spiritual, to mend the church, for Jesus had called them to be fishers of men.

   Mending the lives which are broken is the work of the governmental ministries to the body of Christ. The governmental ministries are to bring those strands that have been broken and battered together with other strands so as to make a strong net which will do the work of catching fish (or souls) for Jesus. When the net broke, James and John did not dive into the water and try to do the work of the net in catching the fish. They were, rather, restoring that part which was broken so that the net itself could function in its work. Pastors in the church are to equip the body to do the work not do the work themselves. (Matthew 4:21)

   b. **Fitted**: Here the Greek word is used to describe the fitting or forming of clay into vessels by a potter. God is the potter who is making vessels of honor or vessels of wrath. A person can respond to the Lord in having his life as pliable clay, or, he can reject the hand of God's shapings. The Lord is the source of all adjustments and corrections. The governmental ministries are His hand to be instruments which the Lord uses to bring that correction. (Romans 9:22)

   c. **Perfectly joined together**: The Corinthian church had been torn from within by the spirit of schism and division. The Apostle Paul's desire was for the church to have all the joints and parts of the body which were out of place to come into adjustment. Paul wanted a mending to take place in the body so that it could function with complete coordination. There is a great need in the church for the five-fold office ministries to be released to their proper function of healing wounds and building again that which has been broken down. The only way that the body of Christ will ever be "perfectly joined together" will be when these ministries are able to fulfill this work in the body. (I Corinthians 1:10)

   d. **Prepared**: The passage quotes a Messianic prophecy found in Psalms 46:6. The body "prepared" for Jesus was a human body of flesh and bones, prepared by the Holy Spirit in Mary's womb. When Jesus came into the world, he came into a "prepared" body for the single purpose of doing the Father's will. As a sinless and perfect body was prepared for the Lord Jesus, so God is preparing a many-membered body through which His Son is continuing His spiritual ministry on the earth. The

Empowering Your Preaching

Father is using the governmental ministries to prepare and perfect the body (the church) so that it can accomplish His eternal purpose of subjugating all things under the feet of Jesus Christ. (Hebrews 10:5)

    e. **Framed**: Here the writer is not talking about the original act of the creating of the worlds, but rather the putting in order, arranging and fitting for use of that which was already existent. The already created worlds were set in order by the Word of God. The universe was adjusted or arranged by God's Word. Similarly, the power of the spoken Word of God will be seen through the governmental ministries as they help to bring the body of Christ together. (Hebrews 11:3)

  3. Classical Greek usages of *Katartismos*
    a. Setting in order a city which had been torn apart by factions and schisms.
    b. The outfitting or preparing of a ship for a long journey.
    c. The preparing of an army for the purpose of battle.

III. THE WORK OF EQUIPPING

  A. Word Pictures to Describe Equippers
    1. Trainers of the soldiers in the army of the Lord
    2. Restorers of the broken bones of the body of Christ
    3. Framers of the boards of God's House
    4. Exercisers of the muscles in Christ's body
    5. Shapers of the stones in the Temple of the Lord
    6. Healers of the breaches in the hedge of God's garden
    7. Liberators of those who are bound
    8. Adjusters of those who are out of joint
    9. Menders of those who are torn
    10. Equippers of the body of Christ
    11. Placers of God's people
    12. Organizers of the Lord's Kingdom
    13. Molders of God's clay vessels
    14. Seers of potential for God's service

  B. Releasing People into their Ministries
    1. Recognize you have the ability and potential
    2. Focus on the positive areas in your life

Pictures of Equippers
1. Trainers of soldiers of God's army
2. Restorers of broken bones of Christ's body
3. Framers of the boards of God's house
4. Exercisers of the muscles of Christ's body
5. Shapers of the stones in God's temple
6. Healers of the breaches in the hedge of God's garden

Pictures of Equippers
7. Liberators of those who are bound
8. Adjusters of those who are out of joint.
9. Menders of those who are torn.
10. Equippers of the body of Christ.
11. Placers of God's people
12. Organizers of the Lord's kingdom
13. Molders of God's clay vessels
14. Seers of potential for God's service

Releasing People Into Their Ministries
1. Recognize you have the ability and potential.
2. Focus on the positive areas of your life.
3. Fulfill your potential and develop your gifts.
4. Be willing to spend time with Jesus and the people of God.
5. Be willing to be frustrated with yourself without giving up on yourself.

Empowering Your Preaching

3. Fulfill your potential and develop your gifts
4. Be willing to spend time with Jesus and the people of God
5. Be willing to be frustrated with yourself without giving up on yourself
6. Encourage yourself through the times of your mistakes
7. Receive a vision in your heart of God's dream for you
8. Take opportunities for development by serving anywhere at all times
9. Put confidence in God and the local church to develop you
10. Pray this ministry into existence

IV. **OBSTACLES TO EQUIPPING**

    A. The Obstacle of Faulty Concepts and Perspective of Pastors and Leaders
        1. The pastor is "Mr. Superstar" and the church is the audience not a body.
        2. The pastor is "Mr. Wonderful" and the church acts as if his faith and abilities were theirs.
        3. Emphasis is on the "Omni-Competent Pastor" not a on multi-gifted body.

    B. The Obstacle of Character and Emotions of Pastors and Leaders
        1. The problem with the more I do the more I'm loved and needed, is that therefore I do everything.
        2. The problem with insecurity is that it drives pastors to do all the work so as to get all the praise.

    C. The Obstacle of Wrong Attitude About Being a Lay Person
        1. David Watson: *"Most Protestant denominations have been as priest-ridden as the Roman Catholics. It is the minister, vicar or pastor who has dominated the whole proceedings. In other words, the clergy-laity divisions have continued in much the same way as in pre-Reformation times, and the doctrine of spiritual gifts and body ministry have been largely ignored."*
        2. John Stott: *"Laity is often a synonym for amateur as opposed to professional, or unqualified as compared to expert."*
        3. The church is fundamentally a charismatic community for the *charismata* (grace gifts) have been distributed to all. This makes each person an initiating center for ministry.

Empowering Your Preaching

    4. Lay-Person - this is a scriptural word filled with dignity and honor, *laos* portrays a sense of specialness. (Dt 7:6; Lev 26:12; I Peter 2:9; Titus 2:14)

    5. A layperson, *laos*, is nothing less than a new humanity, the vanguard of the future, the prototype of the Kingdom of God not yet completed. A person of the future living in the present. Next time you think, *"I'm just a layperson,"* remember, *"That's more than enough!"*

V. THE PROCESS OF BEING EQUIPPED

A. As a believer, you must submit to Christ, making Him lord and laying your life down and receiving from Christ your destiny, your gifts, and your mission in life. (Rom 12:1-2)

> **Process of Being Equipped**
> A. Submit to Christ
> B. Identify with and commit to the local church
> C. Be mended and restored
> D. Be prepared and trained
> E. Be encouraged and released

B. As a believer, you must identify with and commit to the local church body of Christ and the leadership set in that body in order to receive equipping.
    1. Commitment means that I will work through difficulties when they arise instead of running away from them.
    2. Commitment means that I will blend my personal giftings and ministry goals with the vision of that local assembly.
    3. Commitment means that I will give myself faithfully to the members of that church in fellowship and service.
    4. Commitment means that I will invest my time, talents and financial resources to see the vision of my local church become a reality.
    5. Commitment means that I will faithfully gather with my brothers and sisters at the corporate assembling times.
    6. Commitment means that I will take the preached word seriously and make every effort to put it into practice in my life.
    7. Commitment means that I will only do those things that will edify and build up the saints to whom I am joined.
    8. Commitment means that I will honor and respond to those who have oversight in my life as they speak into my life.
    9. Commitment means that I will still support church leadership when policies don't keep to my opinions.
    10. Commitment means that I will utilize personal resources to minister to the needs that God puts in front of me in the local church.

C. The believer, if needed, must be mended and restored personally before they men and restore others. (Luke 4:16)
    1. To fix what is broken. Something is broken when it cannot perform the function for which it has been designed, when it is disjointed or disconnected it must be restored.
    2. Brokenness does not disqualify you from being equipped.

Empowering Your Preaching

D. The believer must be prepared and trained to accomplish his or her God-given task.
1. This takes place after the individual has been properly healed, restored, fixed, and brought to a level of maturity that can handle the disciplines of being discipled for taking responsibility.
2. It is a time of discovering your capacity, aptitudes and abilities for the work of ministry and refining your skills.
3. The church is a training center to help you discover your spiritual gifts and allow you to develop and dispense these gifts. We desire to motivate and fan the flames of desire in you to discover and use your spiritual gifts.
4. Equipping people on every level
    a. Equipping married people to become successful in marriage
    b. Equipping parents to parent biblically and enjoy parenting
    c. Equipping people with the word of God

E. The believer needs to be encouraged and released in their calling and gifting.
1. The Ephesians 4:12 passage clearly states that the saints should <u>do</u>, not just <u>know</u>, the ministry. There is room for all people to take the burden of ministry in the body and out from the body.
2. The eldership and pastoral ministry are here to encourage people as they develop their ministry gifts.

VI. CLOSING (John 17:4; Jer 29:11)

A. Now is the time to be equipped. Don't procrastinate.

B. Identifying Incompletion
1. Things I want to start but I'm not starting.
2. Things I want to change but I'm not changing.
3. Things I want to stop but I'm not stopping.
4. Things I started and I want to finish.
5. Things I want to have but do not have.
6. Things I want to do but have never done.
7. Things I want to be and have never been.

An elderly gentleman sat on a park bench watching a squirrel jump from tree to tree. From the top of one tree, he launched himself towards a limb in another tree that was so far out of reach it appeared to be a suicidal move. Stretching towards the limb, he missed... As he fell short of that branch, the squirrel landed on a lower one, safe and unconcerned. Then he clambered back up to his goal. The old man mused, "Funny. I've seen hundreds of squirrels jump like that, especially when the dogs are roaming around and they can't come down to the ground. A lot of them miss, but I've never seen one hurt by trying." Then he chuckled. "I guess they've got to risk it if they don't want to spend their lives in <u>one tree</u>!"

A Call to Cell Commitment
The Biblical Responsibility of Every Believer

Pastor Frank Damazio

INTRODUCTION. As a pastor/leader, my vision is to plan for an extended future. I know Christ is coming back, but I choose to occupy until that happens, building my life and the life of our church as if we have an extended future! Our vision is to reach people for Christ, lots of them! We live in a metropolitan region with a people drawing power of over 1 million. Churches are to grow. In cities like ours we should see thousands coming to Christ. Large churches small enough to care is the Bible way and our goal. We plan on growing because God loves people and winning people to Christ means discipling them, caring for them and allowing them to enjoy all the benefits of a great church; prayer, worship, communion, equipping, friendship, being cared for biblically. Seoul, Korea has a whopping 750,000 but its size is felt in its 55,000 small groups led by lay people. Bogota, Columbia has 120,000 now with 25,000 small groups. It is possible for us here at City Bible Church to lift the lid off our growth size. Could we think in terms of 5,000 or 10,000 or 20,000 people? The prophetic word to us is seven times a Sunday our church will be filled. It won't change your experience in church. You will still come to one of the seven. You will have a cell group and you will choose your equipping class that may be offered several different times during the week so that you can choose your best night to come. Let us set our vision big. Let us see God do the impossible through us. We must structure for quality growth in both the corporate gathering and in the cells.

City Bible Church Healthy Member Profile: A person who is born again, water baptized and filled with the Spirit, who is faithful to the corporate church gatherings, participates in the cells and School of Equipping; joyfully gives their tithes and offerings, is a pray-er and worshipper, wins people to Christ, has a vision for our region and for world missions, builds a strong family, and loves God with all their heart, soul, mind and strength.

City Bible Church City Cell Profile: A network of relationships that assist in creating a smaller family of believers, each devoted one to another. The City Cell is the primary tool used to provide nurture and care to the entire church body and for believers to share their faith with others, bringing them to Christ. Ultimately each City Cell should be successfully pastoring people, winning the lost, raising new leaders and birthing new cells regularly.

Typical Needs of People in the 21st Century:
1. I still value a personal touch.
2. I want continual options (multiple option choices in ministry programs and service times)
3. Help me to filter today's culture (values questions, time)
4. Enable me to cope with change (living life, decisions, crises)
5. Don't overlook any women (everyone can minister)
6. Capitalize on what motivates me (people's felt needs, multiplicity of people's interests)
7. Show me an organizational structure where people matter.
8. Show me people who care (every tenth member become a care-giver leader)

Empowering Your Preaching

I. **THE TWO GROWTH FACTORS OF THE FIRST CHURCH (Acts 2:46-47)**

   A. The Church at Jerusalem (Acts 1:15; 2:41,47; 4:4; 5:14; 6:7; 21:20)
   1. Very quickly the Jerusalem church's numerical expansion threatened to undo its blessed success. Its quality could continue only if structural reorganization took place.
   2. The Jerusalem church became a meta-church, signifying both a <u>change of mind</u> about how ministry is to be done and a <u>change of form</u> in the infrastructure of the church.

   B. Growth Factor #1: The Balanced Heartbeat of the Corporate and the Cell (Acts 2:46-47)

CORPORATE: Whole Church Gathering	CELL: House to House
1. Celebration	1. Infiltration
2. Preaching	2. Sharing
3. Direction	3. Discipling
4. Equipping	4. Encouraging
5. Building/Edification	5. Expanding/Evangelism

   Corporate: Acts 1:14; 2:11; 2:41; 2:44; Heb 10:24-25; 2 Chr 5:11-14
   Cell: Acts 20:20; Rom 14:7; Heb 3:13; Matt 28:19-20; I Jn 3:14-18; Col 1:28-29

   C. Growth Factor #2: The Identifying and Releasing of Lay Leadership (Acts 6:1-7)

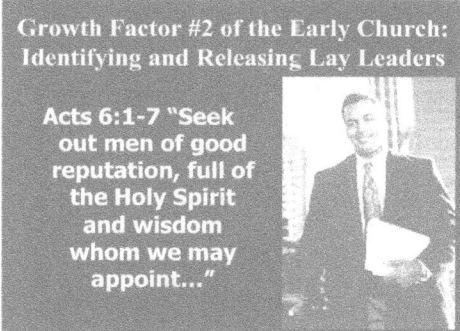

Empowering Your Preaching

II. THE CITY CELL'S DEFINED PURPOSE – A MODEL FOR THE FUTURE

A. Connecting people relationally through small groups.
   1. A small network of believers who are committed to Christ, to biblical values and godly, meaningful relationships. (Acts 2:42-47)
   2. Building relationships in and through the cell obstacles
      a. Unhealthy individualism
      b. Fear of intimate relationships
      c. Fear of loss
      d. Not feeling a personal need to be in a small group

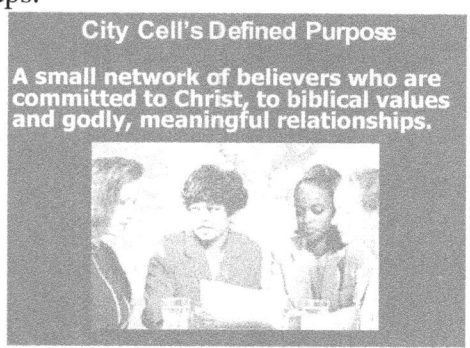

B. Encouraging and equipping every believer to be a disciple of Christ.
   1. The cell is a perfect place to raise up and release every member to function as a responsible Christian.
   2. The cell is a great place to raise up, equip and disciple new converts.
   3. The cell is a great place for releasing people into leadership.
   4. The Holy Spirit has promised to make gifts and gifted people available to churches for mutually edifying one another. (I Cor 12:4-11)
   5. The cell helps a true spiritual formation and disciple making through a rich environment of nurturing care.

C. Learning to use our homes as a ministry center for reaping the harvest.
   1. Natural Progression of Developing a Ministry Perspective
      a. You personally become a ministry center dispensing Christ from your personal treasury.
      b. Your dwelling place becomes a ministry center dispensing love, sacrifice and willingness.
      c. Your neighborhood and immediate areas become your ministry vision with faith and hope.
      d. Your city and metro-plex becomes your larger spiritual responsibility. You care.
   2. Catching the vision of what God might do through your home.
      - "John Wesley had a movement on his hands with much need for outreach, teaching, ministry and leadership and with virtually no ordained clergy at his disposal. The only people available were gifted lay people. As an impressionable boy, he had observed for months the undeniable power of a growing Sunday evening ministry of his own mother, Susanna, as up to 200 people assembled in and outside her Epworth kitchen. She influenced John that lay people were called to preach."

3. Centers of ministry
   a. House of Healing (Mt 8:14-15)
   b. House Open to All (Mt 9:10)
   c. House of Deliverance (Mk 7:30)
   d. House of Salvation (Lk 19:5)
   e. House with Holy Spirit Activity (Acts 2:2)
   f. House of Hospitality (Acts 16:15)
   g. House of Evangelism (Acts 18:7-8)

D. Loosing people from the powers of darkness through united intercessory prayer. (Acts 10:38; Mt 4:12-17; Col 1:13)

E. Strategic creative ministry to impact our immediate geographical areas.
   1. Moving the church into the community (Acts 2:46-47)
   2. Increasing our awareness of needs around us (Mt 9:20-22)
   3. Making unexpected contact with the lost (Ps 2:8)
   4. Invading Satan's territory humbly by God's grace (Acts 17:15-34)
   5. Redeeming the time (Eph 5:16)
   6. Penetrating our streets with righteousness (Acts 19:17-20)
   7. Blessing every place systematically, not a search and destroy mission (Pr 11:11)
   8. When needed, tearing down spiritual strongholds with wisdom (II Cor 10:4)
   9. Praying for spiritual awakening patiently and consistently (Ex 22:30)
   10. Praying for obvious needs of others with compassion and faith (Lk 10:30-35)

III. THE CITY CELL'S BALANCED HEARTBEAT

A. City Cell Life – Describes the shepherding, pastoral, ministry side of the cell. Caring for and ministering to every member through the cell seven days a week. This is the spirit of community or as Acts 2:42 says, *koinonia*, a partnership, generous sharing.

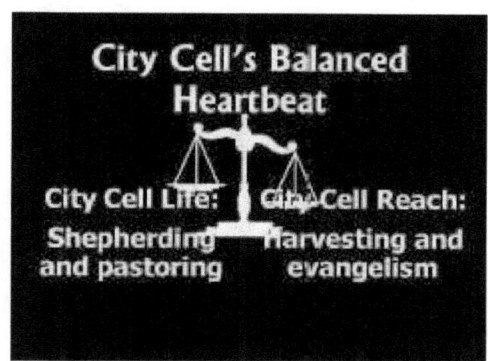

B. City Cell Reach – Describes the harvesting gene within the cell, to be out-reaching not just in-reaching, to apply practically the principles of reaching our city person by person, home by home, neighborhood by neighborhood, thus through the cell seven days a week evangelism will take place.

Empowering Your Preaching

IV. **CELL LEADER DESCRIPTION, REQUIREMENTS AND QUALIFICATIONS**

    A. Seven Basic Marks of a Cell Leader
        1. A disciple of Christ.
        2. A shepherd's heart for the people.
        3. A team player with leadership abilities.
        4. An encourager and equipper.
        5. A discipler of others.
        6. A person of prayer.
        7. A person of faith and vision.

    B. Job Description

The City Cell leader will help facilitate the vision of the church. They will meet bi-monthly with their group and be responsible for all organizational, planning and shepherding of the flock given to their care. To raise up other potential leaders in the group and to mentor them in leading their own City Cell. Lead the City Cell into making an impact in their neighborhoods in bringing the good news of Jesus Christ through prayer and care evangelism.

Empowering Your Preaching

Kingdom Priorities: The Seven "First Things" Given by Jesus

Pastor Frank Damazio

Jesus' Laws of Living

I. **QUESTIONS TO PONDER**

A. Am I really happy, genuinely challenged and fulfilled in life?

B. In light of eternity, am I making a consistent investment for God's glory and cause?

C. Is the direction my life is now taking leading me toward a satisfying and meaningful future?

D. Can I honestly say that I am in the nucleus of God's will for me?

E. Am I communicating godly life goals, a proper value system, a standard of moral purity, a drive for excellence and a commitment to loyalty?

F. Have I discovered the "first things" that push all non-essentials out of my way?

II. **QUOTES AND INSIGHTS FOR LIVING**

A. Stephen Covey, in his book "First Things First Everyday" says, "To live, to love, to learn, to leave a legacy." His famous principle is: "The main thing is to keep the main thing the main thing." What is your main thing in life? What are the first things that push all the non-essentials out of your way?

B. Jesus knew His main thing, His law of firsts. He did not deviate from it. An ancient adage says, "If you want to defeat them, distract them!"

C. **Daniel Webster:** When asked, "What is the greatest thought that can occupy a man's mind?" replied, "His accountability to God."

Empowering Your Preaching

D. **Wayne Martindale:** "Put first things first and we get second things thrown in. Put second things first and we lose both first and second things."

E. **Chuck Swindoll:** "Wisdom is the ability to see with discernment, to view life as God perceives it. Understanding is the skill to respond with insight. Knowledge is the rare trait of learning with perception, discovering and growing. Wisdom is the God-given ability to see with rare objectivity and to handle life with rare stability.

F. In a Peanuts cartoon, Lucy is philosophizing to Charlie Brown. "Charlie Brown, life is a lot like a deck chair. Some place it to see where they've been and some so they can see where they are at the present." Charlie Brown sighs, "I can't even get mind unfolded."

G. Alexander Graham Bell died while dictating a memo in which were written these words, "So little done. So much to do."[1]

H. Snoopy's view of life: "I have a new philosophy. Life is like a golf course ... and a sand trap runs through it."

Putting first things first is an issue at the heart of life. All of us feel torn by the things we want to do, by the demands placed on us, by the many responsibilities we have. Many people today could and do feel disoriented or confused. We may have no real sense of: What are the "first things"? What are the "first" and most important things in my life? Where do I find what is important? What should be my "first things" to live by?

Jesus gives us the wisdom for a life worth living. Jesus is able to summarize for us all of His teachings by using one word: first. Jesus summarizes what is the most important of all His parables, doctrines and stories by giving us seven firsts to live by. He boiled it down, distilled thousands of teachings, writings and theories into the one word: first. If we could grasp our core values, they would save us years of doubts, confusion and misplaced energy. We would live a life with direction and satisfaction. If you want to be happy, do these things. Just as Nike was able to boil it down and pare things down to this essence: Just do it!

III. SEVEN "FIRSTS" SCRIPTURES

A. Matthew 6:33 But seek *first* the kingdom of God and His righteousness, and all these things shall be added to you.

B. Matthew 5:24-25 Leave your gift there before the altar, and go your way. *First* be reconciled to your brother, and then come and offer your gift. Agree with your adversary quickly, while you are on the way with him, lest your adversary deliver you to the judge, the judge hand you over to the officer, and you are thrown into prison.

C. Matthew 7:4-6 Or how can you say to your brother, 'Let me remove the speck from your eye'; and look, a plank is in your own eye? Hypocrite! *First* remove the plank from your own eye, and then you will see clearly to remove the speck out of your brother's eye.

D. Matthew 12:29 Or how can one enter a strong man's house and plunder his goods, unless he *first* binds the strong man? And then he will plunder his house.

E. Matthew 22:36-38 "Teacher, which is the great commandment in the law?" Jesus said to him, " 'You shall love the Lord your God with all your heart, with all your soul, and with all your mind.' This is the *first* and great commandment.

F. Matthew 23:26 Blind Pharisee, *first* cleanse the inside of the cup and dish, that the outside of them may be clean also.

G. Matthew 28:1 Now after the Sabbath, as the *first* day of the week began to dawn, Mary Magdalene and the other Mary came to see the tomb.
- Hebrews 10:25 Not forsaking the assembling of ourselves together, as is the manner of some, but exhorting one another, and so much the more as you see the Day approaching.

IV. **JESUS AND THE LAWS FOR LIVING**

A. The Law of the Single Eye (Mt 6:22-23)

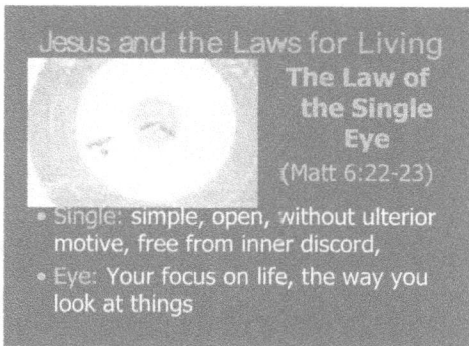

1. Single: *haplous* simple, open, without ulterior motive, wholeheartedly, free from inner discord, innocent, upright, pure

2. The Eye (Proverbs 15:30; Ephesians 1:18)
   - The way of looking at things, your focus on life. You may have an "out of focus" look on life and need to have a single focus. You need to see things from God's point of view, not from a self-centered focus.
   - "If thy desire be single, thy whole personality shall be full of light."

> "Much of our activity these days is nothing more than a cheap anesthetic to deaden the pain of an empty life."

B. The Law of "First Things"

1. First (Gr): first in time and number, first in rank and value, the most important.

2. First (Dictionary): foremost in place, preceding all others in number, the first thing, that which is before anything else. The beginning, the first move, fresh start, starting point, the place of new departure, a new day.

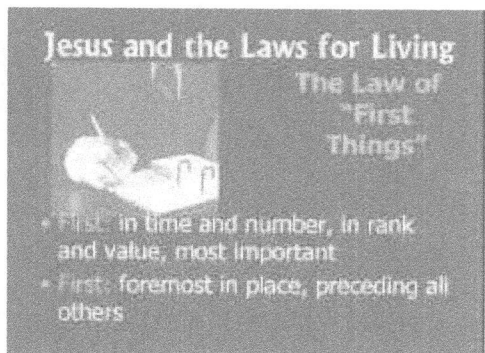

---

[1] Michelle Lovric, <u>Weird Wills & Eccentric Last Wishes</u> (New York: Barnes and Noble, 2000), p. 13

Kingdom Priorities

The Seven "First Things" Given By Jesus

Pastor Frank Damazio

First Seek the Kingdom – Renewing Kingdom Lifestyle

> **Matthew 6:33**
> Set your heart first on His kingdom and His goodness and all these things will come to you as a matter of course.
>
> But you must make His kingdom and uprightness before him your greatest care and all will be yours over and above.

> No one can serve two masters; for either he will hate the one and love the other, or else he will be loyal to the one and despise the other. You cannot serve God and mammon.
> (Matthew 6:24)

- We all struggle
- We all feel the tension
- We all know we want to change
- We all love God and would like to love God more
- Things have changed over time.

Matthew 6:33; Matthew 6:24

INTRODUCTION: A woman once said to E. Stanley Jones, "Dr. Jones, you are obsessed with the kingdom of God." His reply: "I wish that were true because that would be a magnificent obsession." One philosopher said of life appraisal, "An unexamined life is not worth living." We are seeking to appraise our lives by studying the words of Jesus. The seven "firsts" stated by Jesus become a measuring rod for us to evaluate our life quality and life fulfillment. My intention is to ignite your passion for God and to encourage you to return to your first love, Jesus.

- "Much of our activity these days is nothing more than a cheap anesthetic to deaden the pain of an empty life."
- *Knowing is Not Enough*: "Several years ago Dr. Gordon A. Alles, noted chemist who pioneered the development of insulin for the treatment of diabetes, died of that very disease. Friends of Dr. Alles said he either did not know he had the disease or he kept the knowledge to himself. He collapsed in a diabetic coma in his home and died soon after in a local hospital in Pasadena, California. Dr. Alles did considerable research on insulin, helping to purify it sufficiently for human use. Certainly, of all people, he knew how to treat the disease. And if he had knowledge of his own condition, his death was even more tragic. For Dr. Alles, knowing how to treat the disease was not enough."
- *Thomas Kelly on Focus*: "The outer distractions of our interests reflect an inner lack of integration in our own selves. We are trying to be several selves at once without all our selves being organized by a single, mastering Life within us."

Empowering Your Preaching

I. **FIRST SEEK THE KINGDOM OF GOD**

    A. Translations of Matthew 6:33
1. *NKJ*: Seek first the kingdom of God and His righteousness, and all these things shall be added to you.
2. *Amplified*: But seek (aim at and strive after) first of all His kingdom and His righteousness (His way of doing and being right), and then all these things taken together will be given you besides.
3. *Phillips*: Set your heart first on His kingdom and His goodness and all these things will come to you as a matter of course.
4. *Wuest*: But be seeking first the kingdom and His goodness and all these things, all of them, shall be added to you.
5. *Weymouth*: But make His kingdom and righteousness your chief aim and then these things shall all be given you in addition.
6. *Young's Literal*: But seek ye first the reign of God and His righteousness and all these shall be added to you.
7. *Godspeed*: But you must make His kingdom and uprightness before Him, your greatest care and all will be yours over and above.
8. *Barclay*: Make the Kingdom of God and life in loyalty to Him, the object of all your endeavor, and you will get all these other things as well.

    B. The Importance of Renewing a Kingdom Lifestyle

George Barna: "When individuals are single-minded in their devotion to God, then commitment to His ways and His principles becomes much deeper, much more intense. Once they have made an enduring and serious commitment then the peripherals don't matter as much."

1. It shapes our moral and ethical convictions.
2. It directly affects our response to pain and hardship.
3. It gives us strength when we are tempted.
4. It keeps us faithful and courageous when we face impossible odds.
5. It determines our lifestyle and dictates our philosophy.
6. It gives meaning and significance to relationships.
7. It stimulates hope to go on regardless.
8. It aligns our lives with biblical priorities.

Empowering Your Preaching

II. FAR-REACHING EFFECTS OF WHAT WE SEEK FIRST
Read Matthew 6:25-34

- A. The Word Seek
  - The disciples too will seek but they will seek something that is far beyond the thought of the heathen world.
  - Seek: implies a being absorbed in the search for, a persevering and strenuous effort to obtain, be constantly seeking. To seek means on our part, to seek, to obtain and enjoy.

- B. The Wrong Choice: Seeking the wrong things results in worry (Mt 6:25)
  - Worry comes from an old German word meaning to strangle or choke. Worry is a mental and emotional strangulation.
  - Worry is a thin stream of fear that trickles through the mind which, if encouraged, will cut a channel so wide that all other thoughts will be drained out.

    1. *Worry is sin.* It distrusts the promises and providence of God.
    2. *Worry is irreverent.* It fails to recognize God as the master controller of all things.
    3. *Worry is irrelevant.* It does not change things, nor does it help us cope with problems.
    4. *Worry is irresponsible.* It burns up our spiritual energy.
    5. *Worry is the opposite of contentment.* (Phil 4:11-12; I Timothy 6:6-8)
    6. *Worry is unreasonable* because of our faith.
    7. *Worry is setting our hearts on materialism.*

- C. The Right Choice: Seeking the right things results in peace (Mt 6:33)

    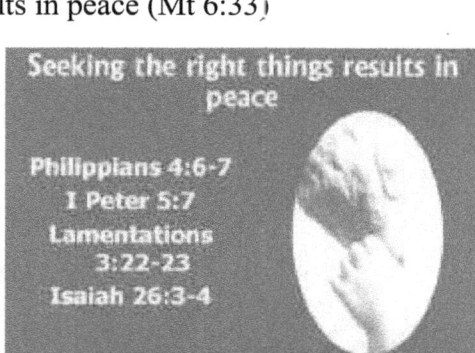

    1. Lenski: He who seeks the kingdom first will seek other things from the father in the right way, by humble and submissive prayer, without worry, without false estimate of these things that are of necessity for living but must be kept in the right place.
    2. Scriptures: Phil 4:6-7; I Peter 5:7; Lamentation 3:22-23; Isaiah 26:3-4
    3. True believers seek first God's kingdom, not simply to refrain from the pursuit of temporal things but to replace such pursuits with goals of greater significance.

Empowering Your Preaching

III. MARKS OR EVIDENCES OF SEEKING FIRST
- Watchman Nee: "A spiritual man is not a man born again, but a man born again and walking in alignment."
- First (Gr): first in time and number, first in rank and value, the most important.
- First (Dictionary): foremost in place, preceding all others in number, the first thing, that which is before anything else. The beginning, the first move, fresh start, starting point, the place of new departure, a new day.

A. To seek first is to place God on the highest place. (Eph 3:17; Mk 12:30)
- The word dwell comes from two words in the Greek. On means "to live in a home" and the other means "down". Paul prays that our Lord might live in our hearts as His home, that He might feel at home in our hearts. "That Christ may finally settle down and feel comfortably at home in your hearts."

> **To seek first is to:**
> 1. Place God on the highest place (Eph 3:17; Mk 12:30)
> 2. Have an appetite for spiritual things (I Cor 2:41-16; 3:1-3)
> 3. To follow God wholeheartedly (Joshua 14:6-14)
> 4. To commune with God first (I Chr 28:9; Is 40:31)

B. To seek first is to have an appetite for spiritual things. (I Cor 2:14-16; 3:1-3)

C. To seek first is to follow God wholeheartedly. (Joshua 14:6-14)
Three times the words "wholly followed" are used to describe a person who had put God first in his life. At the age of 85, Caleb was still spiritually alert, committed, ready for the challenge. He lived for God wholeheartedly with nothing held back. What kind of an old man do you want to be?

D. To seek first is to commune with God first. (I Chr 28:9; Is 40:31)
Devotion belongs to the inner life and lives in the closet. It belongs to the person whose thoughts and feelings are devoted to God and who possesses a strong affection for God. This is the genesis of the whole matter of activity and strength of the most energetic, exhaustless and untiring nature. All this is the result of waiting on God.

E. To seek first is to follow and honor Jesus in everything I do. (Phil 1:20-21; Mk 11:29-30)
- ***Thomas Kempis*** (a German mystic): "But whoever would fully and feelingly understand the words of Christ must endeavor to conform his life wholly to the life of Christ."
- "What Would Jesus Do" bracelets, the book "In His Steps."

> **To seek first is to:**
> 5. To follow and honor Jesus in everything I do (Phil 1:20-21; Mk 11:29-30)
> 6. To remove all the clutter in my life (Rom 12:1-2)
> 7. To be ambitious for God's purposes, setting self aside (Acts 20:24)

Empowering Your Preaching

F. To seek first is to remove all the clutter in my life. (Rom 12:1-2)
- Aiden Wilson Tozer (1897-1963): A country boy who, without formal education, became one of the greatest American pastors and leader of Southside Alliance Church in Chicago from 1928 – 1959. As pastor, he did virtually no administrative work or pastoral counseling. He spent his time in prayer, meditation and the word. His books are many.
- **Prayer by A.W. Tozer:** "Father, I want to know thee, but my coward heart fears to give up its toys. I cannot part with them without inward bleeding, and I do not try to hide from Thee the terror of the parting. I come trembling, but I do come. Please root from my heart all those things which I have cherished so long and which have become a very part of my living self, so that Thou mayest enter and dwell there without a rival. Then shalt Thou make the place of Thy feet glorious. Then shall my heart have no need of the sun to shine in it, for Thyself wilt be the light of it, and there shall be no night there. In Jesus' name, Amen."[1]
- Clutter of unnecessary activities, things, habits, attitudes.

G. To seek first is to be ambitious for God's purposes, setting self aside. (Acts 20:24)
William Booth, co-founder of the Salvation Army: "One of his biographers tells of the day when the general was in his eighties. He was ill and had been to see a physician. It was left to his son, Bramwell, to tell him that he would soon be blind. "You mean that I am going blind?" "Well, General, I fear that we must contemplate that," said Bramwell, who along with the family had always addressed their father by that affectionate name. There was a pause while Booth thought over what he had been told. And then the father asked the son, "I shall never see your face again?" "No, probably not in this world," was the son's reply. The biographer writes, "During the next few moments the veteran's hand crept along the counterpane to take hold of his son's, and holding it he said very calmly, 'God must know best!' And after another pause, 'Bramwell, I have done what I could for God and for the people with my eyes. Now I shall do what I can for God and for the people without my eyes.'"[2]

H. To seek first is to give God the priority that is His due. (Phil 3:13-14)

I. To seek first is to seek first His rule, His will and His authority. (Col 1:13-14)

J. To seek first is to be in complete submission to the Holy Spirit in both decisions and behavior. (Ezek 36:26-27; John 14:15-16; Eph 5:18-19; Gal 5:25)

> To seek first is to:
> 8. To give God the priority that is His due (Phil 3:13-14)
> 9. To seek first His rule, His will and His authority (Col 1:13-14)
> 10. To be in complete submission to the Holy Spirit (Ezek 36:26-27)
> 11. To have a heart sensitive to sin (Eph 4:30)

K. To seek first is to have a heart sensitive to sin and anything that offends God. (Eph 4:30)

---

[1] Charles R. Swindoll. The Tale of the Tardy Oxcart (Nashville: Word Publishing, 1998), p. 308.
[2] Gordon MacDonald. The Life God Blesses (Nashville: Thomas Nelson Publishers, 1994), pp. 65-66.

Seven Power Points of Prayer
Preparation and Hindrances to Prayer

by Pastor Frank Damazio

Isaiah 56:7; Matthew 21:13; Hosea 10:12

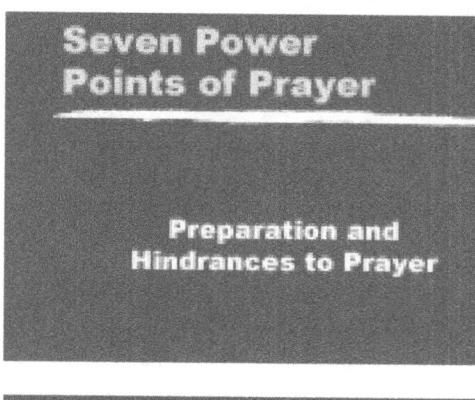
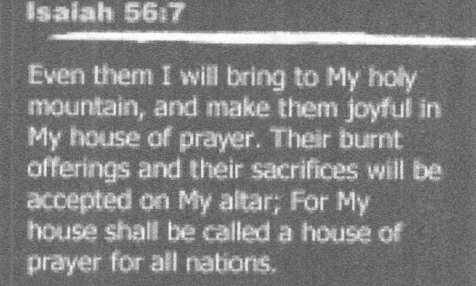
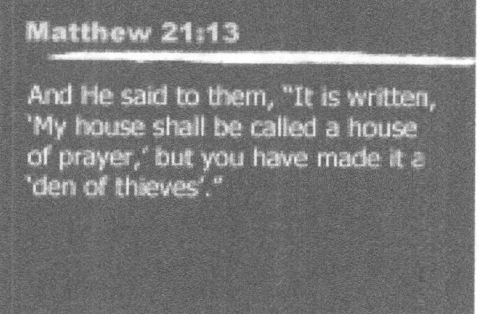

INTRODUCTION: A spirit of revival or renewal in the hearts of true believers should always result in a renewed spirit of prayer. We have always been a church who held to the doctrine of prayer; now our desire is to increase the *spirit* of prayer in our church. Let us walk in that truth with more power than ever. A praying church is a church that moves deeper into strategic and consistent prayer. Prayer can be dynamic and exciting or dull and deadly. It is simple and yet complex. It is natural and yet a skill to be learned. The church may be a well-oiled machine with its intricate parts—all sizes and shapes—placed together and designed to work smoothly, yet without lubrication these parts will destroy each other. Prayer is God's oil of lubrication for His church.

Praying with heart, with deep feelings. Nurture a spirit of prayer from a life chamber, life spirit. Feel deeply about what we express. AIDS is only the name of a disease until we know someone, a friend, who has it. The same with cancer, divorce, barrenness. The Pharisees prayed from the head, not the heart. Jesus spoke a strong word to them. "Your lips draw night but your heart is far from me."

Empowering Your Preaching

> Sow for yourselves righteousness; reap in mercy; break up your fallow ground, for it is time to seek the LORD, till He comes and rains righteousness on you. (Hosea 10:12)

Break up	=	preparation
Unplowed ground	=	hindrance
Time	=	urgency
Seek the Lord	=	focus
Until	=	persistence
He comes	=	power of presence
Showers rain	=	abundant answers

In this verse we have discovered seven power points of prayer. The verse, studied word by word, yields these seven points:

1. Preparation of prayer
2. Hindrances to prayer
3. Urgency of prayer
4. Seekers school of prayer
5. Persistence of prayer
6. Dynamic presence of prayer
7. Abundant answers to prayer

The Preparation for Prayer
Break Up
- A biblical command (Isaiah 18:5; Leviticus 25:5; Isaiah 5:6)
- A personal commitment
- A work of labor
- A work of sacrifice
- A work of perseverance
- A work of renovation

I. THE PREPARATION FOR PRAYER—" BREAK UP" (Job 16:12; Ps 31:12; Mt 21:42-44)

   A. "Break Up" is a biblical command. (Isaiah 18:5; Lev 25:5; Is 5:6)

   1. Defining the phrase: Over ten different Hebrew words and ten different Greek words are rendered "break" in the Bible.

   2. Break Up means: a shattering, penetrating; to split something asunder, to divide, to open what is shut; to lay open anything closed that it may break forth; to break in or penetrate, even by force; to smite or strike with a hammer; to till, to cultivate as preparing for sowing seed into soil; to break clods into small pieces.

   3. Break up your heart and mind, preparing your mind, heart and spirit to bring forth fruit unto God

   4. How? Remove by repentance, confession, cleansing the sins that have and are hardening the heart: ingratitude, neglect, coldness, worldly mindedness, pride, unforgiveness, slander, lying, jealousy, temper

5. Pruning
   a. Cutting back will head off growth in wrong directions.
   b. Good pruning cuts the shoots that sap the strength.
   c. To cut away useless shoots.
   d. Removal of dead wood that could have decay or disease.
   e. Removal of living wood. An untrimmed vine develops long branches that use the strength needed for fruit to develop the branches.

B. "Break up" is a personal commitment

1. Break up is a <u>work of labor</u> (for which the master imparts strength)

2. Break up is a <u>work of sacrifice</u> (for which the Lord communicates fortitude)

3. Break up is a <u>work of perseverance</u> (for which the Lord of the soil supplies patience)

4. Break up is a <u>work of renovation</u> (for which the owner of the ground affords means. The soil in its present state is unfit to produce any useful crop, but when the weeds are destroyed the ground shall be renewed that it may bring forth good fruit)

II. THE HINDRANCE TO PRAYER – "UNPLOWED GROUND"

A. The Unplowed Ground

1. *Unproductive soil*: produces nothing, it is not like soil or field which never has produced anything for this ground has had its crops and has been fruitful!

2. *Untilled soil*: is destitute of the fruit it might produce, neglected, left fallow unintentionally yet by temptation, negligence and ignorance

3. *Unprofitable soil*:
   a. Those whose affections, habits, thoughts were once bearing a rich harvest for God but in whom this is all changed and the heart has become barren.
   b. The foul, hard, unprofitable soil of the carnal, natural man must be broken up. Hard clods broken by the plough.
   c. Wastefulness, uncultivated earth with weeds, thistles, thorns, unfruitfulness. Sun, dew, rain—all fall in vain.

B. Discerning the Present Condition of the Heart
(Matthew 13:1-9; 13:18-23)
- This parable shows that the sower expects fruit and knows that the variety of soils will determine the crop.

1. <u>Indifferent</u>: a heart hardened by busyness or preoccupation (Mt 13:19; Lk 14:17-20). "Seeds path".

a. Allows the word to be lost from memory while other things receive more attention on the beaten path of life
   b. Greek: the paths along the edge of a plowed field. The beaten paths. "One who listens but not comprehends."
   c. Some people hear the word, but like hardened paths, do not let the truth penetrate. Before they really understand it, the devil has snatched it away.

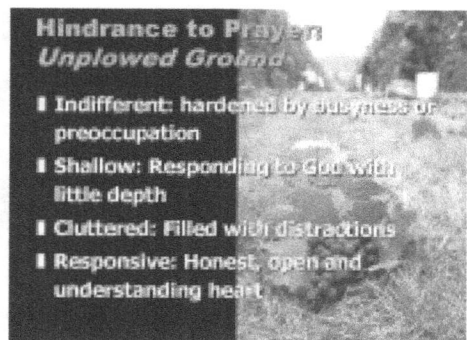

2. <u>Shallow</u>: responding to God with little depth (Mt 13:20). "Rocky places".

   a. Has a hidden agenda and other priorities which prevent in-depth understanding.

   b. Receives the word in a superficial, thoughtless way and shows immediate signs of life and promises to be the best crop. External pressures, trouble, persecution reveal the shallowness of this soil. Temporary disciple, temporary growth.

   c. No roots, temptation, immediately offended. Limestone country, layered rock with thin covered soil upon the layers of rock, seed "shot up at once" but had no roots. Offended in the Greek means he is quickly snared.

3. <u>Cluttered</u>: a crowded heart filled with distractions (Mt 13:22) "Thorny ground": It is a heart that has good potential but is full of distractions.

   a. Lives are filled with the interests of this world and their materialistic ambitions choke out the convictions for the kingdom.

   b. Never permits the message of the word to control him. Life has too many other commitments that slowly choke the struggling plant which never matures and bears fruit. The competing thorns are summed up under two headings: worries of life and deceitfulness of riches (Greek: delight in riches). Thorns are so subtle that one may not be aware of the choking that is going on.

   c. This person finds all the seeming good effect is gone leaving the soil a very thicket of thorns.

   d. Choking: This is a slow process. In the Greek it means to press round or

throng one so as almost to suffocate. To seize a person's throat. It is used metaphorically of the "crowding thorns" preventing growth.

    e. Cares, riches, lusts of other things: these all choke the word. The seeds of thorns are already in the ground. Martha syndrome: pot is on the stove, kids are coming home from school, boss is on the phone, car needs fixing... Make room in our spirits!

4. <u>Responsive</u>: an honest, open and understanding heart (Mt 13:23). "Good soil."

    a. Welcomes the word; hungers and thirsts after righteousness; longs for the meaning of right purpose.

    b. The condition of receiving God's revelation and of holding God's truth is one of the heart, not one of the head. The ability to receive and search out is like that of the child, the synonym of docility, innocence and simplicity. These are the conditions on which God reveals himself to men. The world by wisdom cannot know God, can never receive nor understand God, because God reveals himself to men's hearts not to their heads. Only hearts can ever know God and feel God, can see God and can read God in His book of books. God is not grasped by thought but by feeling. The world gets God by revelation, not by philosophy. It is not apprehension (the mental ability to grasp God), but plasticity (the ability to be impressed) that men need. It is not by hard, strong, stern, great reasoning that the world gets a hold of God but by big, soft, pure hearts. Not so much do men need light to see God as they need hearts to feel God!

    c. Healthy spiritual inner attitudes which easily receive and retain the things spoken by the Spirit, whether directly or by the preached word. A sensitivity to the Holy Spirit.

    d. Understanding Heart: In the Hebrew the basic idea is that of perceiving a message, attentive, to hear and perceive, to hear and obey, quality of hearing, hearing clearly, to gain insight by hearing, discernment, to distinguish between, leads to understanding. The seat of insight is the heart which discerns the work and word of God.

The Church Called to Intercession
Responding to the Call of the Spirit to Become a Church of Intercession

Pastor Frank Damazio

Ezekiel 22:30; 13:5; Matthew 16:18

INTRODUCTION: We are endeavoring to lay a deep and broad foundation as we build a house of intercessory prayer. This is a vital link to our future and the force behind our vision. As a church, we are responding to the call of the Spirit to become a church of intercession, not only special intercessors but a congregation of priests who know how to burn their spiritual incense. This is a high calling. Every believer is a member of an occupational force which has one principle purpose: to enforce the victory of Calvary. This is the context of prayer. More than a single dimensional asking, prayer becomes a multi-faceted weapon through supplication, intercession, travail and thanksgiving.

OUR GOAL: To motivate the entire congregation into a deeper level of prayer and intercession that would release the supernatural powers of God in an obvious and awesome manner, resulting in awesome harvest.

Empowering Your Preaching

- John Maxwell: In <u>Six Keys to Church Growth</u> the number one key is a praying church. "Every time I have had a breakthrough in the growth and life of my church it has been because of intentional intercessory prayer."
- Bob Logan (Consultant on church growth): Seven most important things I have learned in church planting, #1 church intercessory prayer. Prayer is not preparation for the battle. Prayer is the battle.
- Waymon Rodgers: The ministry of prayer is the most important of all the ministries in the church. Prayer creates the atmosphere and binds the powers of darkness to the gospel of Jesus can go forward and the church can prosper.

I. **GOD SEEKS FOR INTERCESSORS**
   Ezekiel 22:30; 13:5

   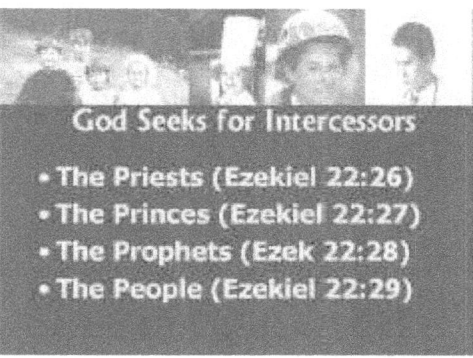

   A. The Priests -- *Ezekiel 22:26*

   B. The Princes -- *Ezekiel 22:27*

   C. The Prophets -- *Ezekiel 22:28*

   D. The People -- *Ezekiel 22:29*

II. **GOD SEEKS FOR INTERCESSORS TO BUILD HEDGES**

   A. The Hedge: Hebrew definition: To surround with a fence or a wall; to protect; to set anyone in trouble, distress or danger in a safe place; to keep out the enemies of the vineyard, the flock, the city or the house.

   B. The Hedge Broken Down

   1. Broken down hedge allows <u>satanic attack</u> (Ecclesiastes 10:8)

   2. Broken down hedge allows <u>God's vineyard to be trampled</u> (Isaiah 5:5)

   3. Broken down hedge allows <u>fruit to be ruined</u> (Psalm 80:12)

   4. Broken down hedge allows <u>seats of Satan to be established in our city</u> (Psalm 89:40)

   C. The Hedge Restored, Rebuilt, Repaired (Job 1:10; Isaiah 62:6)

   1. Social bondage sites -- Strongholds of community suffering, destabilizing social values and destructive vices. Examples include crack houses, nightclubs, gang hideouts, abortion clinics, pornography shops and theaters.

Empowering Your Preaching

2. "...An oppression over this city that the Lord is going to use this house to break. An oppression of poverty, of addiction. The alcohol, the demonic oppression that has crept in and stolen the heritage of God's people in this city shall be broken, saith the Lord. It's the house of the Lord, under the anointing of the Spirit, that shall break the yoke and bring deliverance to this city, saith the Lord." (Prophetic Assembly April ,1996)

III. GOD SEEKS FOR INTERCESSORS TO STAND IN THE GAP

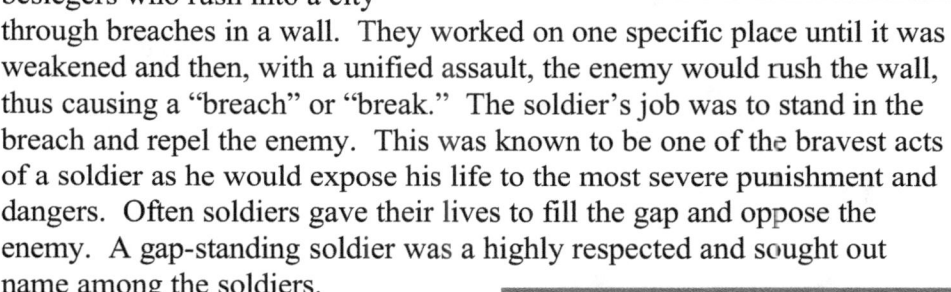

A. The Gap
  1. Hebrew Definition: a rupture, a breach
  2. This word is taken from military contexts. It is the picture of besiegers who rush into a city through breaches in a wall. They worked on one specific place until it was weakened and then, with a unified assault, the enemy would rush the wall, thus causing a "breach" or "break." The soldier's job was to stand in the breach and repel the enemy. This was known to be one of the bravest acts of a soldier as he would expose his life to the most severe punishment and dangers. Often soldiers gave their lives to fill the gap and oppose the enemy. A gap-standing soldier was a highly respected and sought out name among the soldiers.

B. Repairing and Standing in the Gap
   Psalm 106:23; Isaiah 58:12; I Kings 11:27

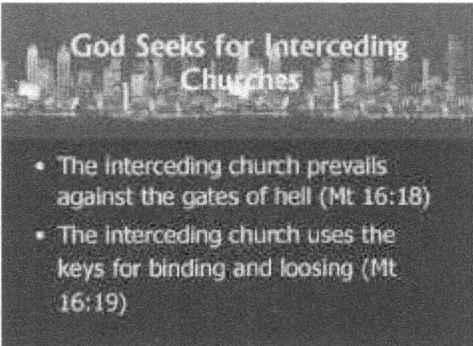

IV. GOD SEEKS FOR INTERCEDING CHURCHES

A. The Interceding Church Prevails Against the Gates of Hell

  1. Matthew 16:18 "I will build my church and the gates of hell shall not prevail."
     - "The power and forces of death shall never overpower the church."
     - "And the locks of Sheol shall not shut on it."
     - "And the power of the underworld shall never overthrow it."
     - "And the gates of hell shall not hold out against it."
     - "The power and government of Hades will never be able to resist the church."

Empowering Your Preaching

      2.   Gates: The function of gates is to keep things in, confine them, shut them up, control them. The gates are the counsels of darkness, the plots, ploys and plunderings of satanic origin which are spawned in the spirit realm and erupt in the physical. (Isaiah 26:2; 60:11)

B.   The Interceding Church Uses the Keys for Binding and Loosing
Matthew 16:19 "I will give you the keys of the kingdom of heaven and whatever you shall bind on earth shall be bound."

      1.   Keys are given to the church to stop hell's worst, to unlock prison doors, to shatter Satan's chains. Keys represent the authority one has to enter certain domains. God is giving the church the right to function in the domains of the Almighty.

      2.   To bind is to intercede
          a.   Bind is the Greek word *deses*. Supplication is the Greek word *deesis*.
          b.   Binding is contracting with God through intercessory prayer saying, "Father, what you have willed I call forth upon earth."
          c.   Binding is a steadfast continuity in regular and unceasing prayers, indicating a timeless pursuit of a given goal.
          d.   Binding is an intense spiritual struggle in which the issue will determine, with far reaching effect, the whole work of the kingdom of God.

Luke 1;13; 2:37; 5:33; Acts 1:14; Romans 10:1; II Corinthians 1:11; 9:14; Ephesians 6:18; Philippians 1:4; 1:19; 4:6; II Timothy 2:1; 5:5; II Timothy 1:3; Hebrews 5:7; James 5:16; I Peter 3:12

> "Whenever you determine to lay claim to the Father's counsels as opposed to the adversary's, you'll find that earth can have what heaven has already decided on!"

TWELVE REWARDS OF A RENEWED SOUL
An Exposition of Psalm 23

by Pastor Frank Damazio

The Reward of Renewed Faith in God's Divine Provision

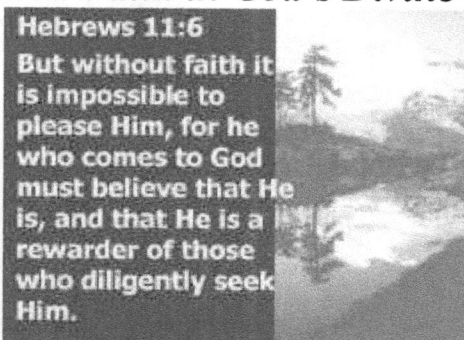

Heb 11:6 But without faith it is impossible to please Him, for he who comes to God must believe that He is, and that He is a rewarder of those who diligently seek Him.

INTRODUCTION: This psalm of the renewed soul is for each individual believer. God is your God. Take the words of this psalm on your lips and express gratitude and confidence that all the demonstrations of God's covenant love are yours. This is a pastoral psalm, one that seeks intimate trust in God. It does not just provoke our thinking; it touches below our philosophy and our theology and comes to us like a cover for the heart, a refuge from weariness, a shelter from the rain.

The Lord is My Shepherd

1. Lord = (Hebrew) Yahweh: name speaks of the provision and protection of the covenant-making and covenant keeping God. It always connotes God's ability to always be absolutely faithful to His people. Jehovah: I will be all that is necessary as the need arises.

2. My = personal, individual

3. Psalm 23:1 Yahweh is my shepherd. He provides!
   ...I shall not lack
   ...I don't need a thing
   ...I shall lack nothing
   ...I shall never be in need
   ...I will not be without any good thing
   ...I have everything I need
   ...I shall not suffer any want

Empowering Your Preaching

I. **THE FAITH OPTIMISM FACTOR**
   "I" shall not want. Not *us* or *they*, but *I, me*.

   A. Moving from Knowledge Faith to Experiential Personal Faith (Mt 9:27-29)
      Developing an attitude of faith, optimism, possibility for God to work!

      1. Moving from doctrinal faith to an attitude of faith (I Samuel 17:37)

      2. Moving away from pessimism to true biblical faith optimism
         - Pessimism expects the worst of God and life. Faith is exceedingly hopeful, trusting and confident!

      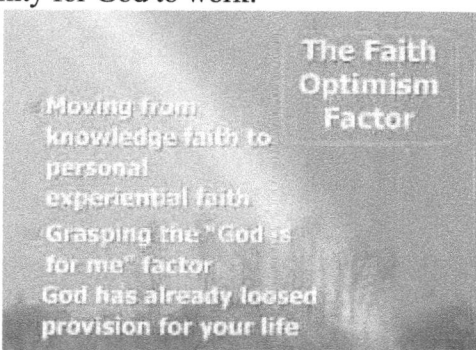

   B. Grasping the "God is For Me" Factor
      Optimistic expectation about receiving help from God.

      1. God knows everything about our circumstance
         - If God has proven trustworthy in one circumstance, He can be trusted in another!

      2. God has already decided to help you. (II Chronicles 16:9)

   C. God has already released His provisions toward your life. Take them!

      1. Blind Bartimaeus (Mk 10:46-52)

      2. Woman with the Hemorrhage (Mk 5:23-34)

II. **THE PROVISION FACTOR**
   "I shall not want."

   A. Hebrew:
      Haser = to be in poverty, needy, lacking
      Hoser = to be in want, to lack
      Hesron = deficiency

      1. Most frequently used to express the sufficiency of God's grace to meet the needs of His people. They never lack.

      2. Translated in English: lacked, wanted, waters abated, waters decreased, no need, should fail

      3. I shall not live in spiritual poverty; I shall not lack His abundance in my life; I shall not live in deficiency but in His sufficiency.

Empowering Your Preaching

B. Seven Confessions of a Renewed Faith (Dt 2:7; 8:9; Neh 9:21)

1. Shall not lack wisdom, understanding. (Hos 4:6)

   a. Those who lack godly wisdom:
   1) Commit foolish sins (Pr 6:32)
   2) Belittle their neighbors (Pr 11:12)
   3) Rejoice over folly (Pr 15:21)
   4) Make foolish vows (Pr 17:18)
   5) Sluggards with a field (Pr 24:30)
   6) Poor leader who oppresses (Pr 28:16)

   b. If one realizes this lack, he can gain wisdom by looking to the provider of wisdom. (Pr 9:4,16; James 1:6)

   c. C.S. Lewis said of the wisdom of man: "No clever arrangement of bad eggs will make a good omelet."

2. Shall not lack miracle provisions for living (Exodus 16:18; Isaiah 32:6; Ezekiel 4:17; II Kings 4:3)
   a. Don't put limitations on God's ability to provide.
   b. God works through our positive expectations and faith to do great things.
   c. God works through strange vessels to bring supernatural provision. God sent the ravens, unclean birds, to bring food to Elijah.

3. Shall not lack honor (I Cor 12:23-24; Prov 22:4; 31:25; 27:18; John 8:54; I Tim 5:17)

4. Shall not lack spiritual perspective, perception or clear vision (II Peter 1:9)

5. Shall not lack faith and trust in the midst of fiery trials (I Thess 3:10; II Corinthians 1:4; II Peter 1:7-9; James 1:12)

6. Shall not lack divine guidance for my life (Psalm 32:8; 48:14; Isaiah 58:11)

7. Shall not lack supernatural peace in the midst of crisis (Philippians 4:7-9; Colossians 3:15; II Thessalonians 3:16)
   a. Peace that passes all understanding
   b. No worry. "Worry has been defined as a small trickle of fear that meanders through the mind until it cuts a channel into which all other thoughts are drained!"

Empowering Your Preaching

The Unsearchable Riches of Christ
The Riches of Mercy

Pastor Frank Damazio

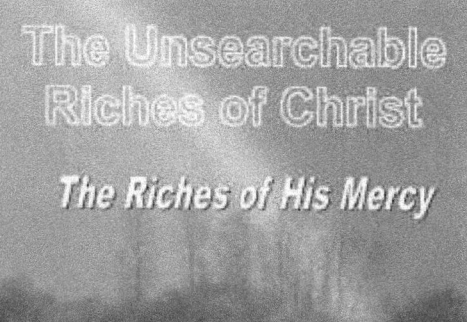

> To me, who am less than the least of all the saints, this grace was given, that I should preach among the Gentiles the **unsearchable riches of Christ**.
> (Ephesians 3:8)

INTRODUCTION: The riches and treasures found in Christ become the believer's treasures. Christ is the storehouse of all spiritual riches. We must, by faith, receive from His storehouse the riches of grace, mercy and glory. In the Greek, "riches" means to fill until full, the fullness of precious goods, to have in abundance, to be enriched spiritually. (II Corinthians 6:10; II Corinthians 8:9)

Riches in Ephesians
1. The Riches of Grace, *Ephesians 1:7; 2:7*
2. The Riches of Mercy, *Ephesians 2:4*
3. The Riches of Glory, *Ephesians 3:16*

> ***The Riches of Mercy***
> But God, who is rich in mercy, because of His great love with which He loved us (Ephesians 2:4).

I. **MERCY: A RICH WORD INDEED**

   A. Old Testament Hebrew Words in the Mercy Family

   1. Hesed: This Hebrew word, found 250 times in the Old Testament, is predominantly translated by the English word "mercy". It also is translated kindness, lovingkindness, and goodness. It denotes devotion to a covenant, thus is used of God's covenant love. Hesed is a strong word of covenant love, the picture of one who (despite his unworthiness and defection) is readily passed over into God's mercy. Hesed is the steady, persistent refusal of God to wash His hands of wayward people. His love is steadfast and enduring. This is hesed.
   Esther 2:17; Deuteronomy 7:9; 7:12

2. **Hanan**: This Hebrew word is translated have mercy upon, be gracious, merciful, grace and favor. It is the gracious favor of the superior to the inferior, all undeserved.

3. **Racham**: This is the Hebrew word that shares common origin with "rechem" meaning womb, hence brotherly or motherly feelings. This word denotes tender mercies and expresses the affective aspect of love, its compassion and pity.

B. New Testament Mercy Is Love
Agape is the word used to describe the way God loves. It is totally different from the love that seeks its own fulfillment or the carnal passion of finding satisfaction in using another for one's benefit. Agape love seeks no self-fulfillment, is not based on the worthiness of the object, loves the unlovely, unbeautiful, even the repulsive. It is a love that gets nothing in return, that loves even when resisted or rejected. It is a love that, regardless of the worth or response of the object, keeps giving itself.

C. Biblical View of Mercy
- Exod 34:6-7; Heb 4:16; Deut 5:10; Hab 3:2; Titus 3:5; Ps 18:25; Ps 41:4; Luke 18:13

II. MERCY -- THE ESSENCE OR SUBSTANCE OF MERCY

A. Mercy is when someone who is in the position of helper and doer so while unexpected and undeserved by the recipient. No one has a right to mercy. When we understand this fact and its implications, we gain a deeper appreciation of God's goodness to us.

B. Mercy Ingredients

1. **Merciful** – To be inclined toward, favorably inclined, to favor someone, to give them what they need, to love unconditionally. (*Psalm 18:25; 41:4; Luke 18:13*)

2. **Gracious** – To show special tenderness toward, to treat with gentleness, carefulness; heartfelt response by someone who has something to give to one who has a need; to bend. (*Nehemiah 9:17; 9:31; Psalm 86:15; I Peter 2:3*)

- **Merciful**: To be favorably inclined toward someone and give them what they need
- **Graciousness**: To show special tenderness to someone who is in need
- **Longsuffering**: To be slow to anger

- As Gandhi stepped aboard a train one day, one of his shoes slipped off and landed on the track. He was unable to retrieve it as the train was moving. To the amazement of his companions, Gandhi calmly took off his other shoe and threw it back along the track to land close to the first. Asked by a fellow passenger why he did so, Gandhi smiled. "The poor man who finds the shoe lying on the track," he replied, "will now have a pair he can use."[1]

Empowering Your Preaching

3. **Longsuffering** – To be slow to anger, make long, to prolong. *(Ps 86:15; I Peter 3:20)*
   - **Story of Little Annie:** Years ago, in the Boston Mental Hospital, lived a very disturbed young girl named, "Little Annie." She was labeled, "hopeless" due to her extreme condition, which included, frequent violent acts, biting, scratching, cussing, which often time brought danger to herself as well as others. She was heavily medicated and rarely visited by anyone………except one elderly nurse.

     She would visit Little Annie daily taking two fresh cookies on a plate with a cup of milk. Annie would pull her hair, spit on her, scream and create unusually uncomfortable situations, but the elderly nurse would not give up. Everyday she would return to find the Little Annie did not touch any of the cookies. She would simply replace two new cookies for the two old ones.

     After six months of verbal and physical abuse, the nurse was amazed to see that when she returned, one of the cookies were gone. She knew that she was getting somewhere! Months later the spitting stopped. Next the scratching and screaming stopped. There was miracles happening each week.

     Years later, when Little Annie turned eighteen years of age, they felt that she could be released, as they felt she had become a productive member of society. Her reply was, " I want to dedicate my entire life to helping others just as I have been helped by my dearest friend, my nurse."

     Little Annie went on to devoting her life to serving others. Her real name, Annie Sullivan, the lady who trained and educated Helen Keller.

4. **Goodness** – To go beyond what is expected in order to give kindness, wealth, health, happiness. *(Romans 2:4; Psalm 52:1; 65:4; 107:8-9)*
   - **Story of Jerry Burdett:** Jerry Burdett was a man you probably never heard of, but will go down in history as one of the most heroic and selfless persons who ever lived. One windy day while strolling down the beach with his beautiful wife enjoying each other's company, there was a series of faint screams in the distance. Immediately they focused their attention out in the ocean to a group of three people who had been caught in a riptide and pulled swiftly out to sea. Due to the choppy water and the swells of the ocean, the voices showed signs of fatigue and urgency. Jerry looked at his wife, threw off his coat and shoes and dove into the water swimming rapidly towards the drowning people.

     - Goodness: To go beyond what is expected in order to give kindness to someone
     - Compassion: To cherish with gentle affection
     - Kindness: To do good, kind acts of love
     - Sympathy: To be affected with the same feeling as another

     Within minutes he grabbed a hold of the most fatigued person and labored to bring them close to the shore where they could stand. Taking a deep breath and looking quickly at his wife, he turned and dove into the next large crashing wave to swim back out to save the next person. In a matter of minutes Jerry and the next person were in view and he brought them within safe waters.

     Jerry was extremely drained and completely incapable of another rescue attempt, but was driven by the shrieks and cries of both the people on the shore

and the last person out in the sea. He then made a decision that would affect his life and his families forever, he dove into the next crashing wave to save the last person. Minutes passed by, people stood on the shore holding their breath, even some praying for their safety. A large wave came crashing in and out of the foam popped two heads, as Jerry was laboring to bring this person to safety. It was at that point that the person being rescued gave a last attempt to lung towards the shore and was stripped from the stronghold of the riptide. Jerry, being completely exhausted, took a breath to dip under the next crashing wave. As the next series of waves settled, Jerry was no where in sight. Jerry gave his life so that others might live.

5. Compassion – To be soft, soothing, cherishing, gentle affection; behold with tenderness. (*Psalm 103:8; 111:4; 112:4; Lamentations 3:22*)
   - "On the street I saw a small girl cold and shivering in a thin dress with little hope of a decent meal. I became angry and said to God: 'Why did you permit this? Why don't you do something about it?' For awhile God said nothing. That night he replied, quite suddenly: 'I certainly did something about it. I made you.'"[2]

6. Kindness – Moral goodness, integrity; opposed to harsh, hard, bitter or sharp; to desire to do good; kind acts of love; do something pleasant (*Ephesians 2:7; Ruth 3:10; Psalm 31:21; 117:2; Titus 3:4*)

7. Sympathy – To be affected with the same feeling as another, to sympathize with; to feel for or have compassion on; to come quickly to one's help. (*Hebrews 4:15; Matthew 9:21*)
   - Author and lecturer Leo Buscaglia once talked about a contest he was asked to judge. The purpose of the contest was to find the most caring child. The winner was a four-year-old child whose next-door neighbor was an elderly gentleman who had recently lost his wife. Upon seeing the man cry, the little boy went into the old gentleman's yard, climbed onto his lap and just sat there. When his mother asked him what he had said to the neighbor, the little boy said, "Nothing. I just helped him cry."[3]

---

[1] Jack Canfield, Mark Victor Hansen. A 2nd Helping of Chicken Soup for the Soul. (Deerfield Beach, FL: Health Communications, Inc., 1995), pg. 5.
[2] Jack Canfield, Mark Victor Hansen, Patty Aubery and Nancy Mitchell. Christian Soup for the Christian Soul. (Deerfield Beach, FL: Health Communications, Inc., 1997), pg. 40.
[3] Jack Canfield and Mark Victor Hansen. A Third Serving of Chicken Soup for the Soul. (Deerfield Beach, FL: Health Communications, Inc., 1996), pg 12.

Empowering Your Preaching

We Can Touch The World
Building Bridges to Reach Local, National and International People to Receive Christ and Biblical Resources

Pastor Frank Damazio

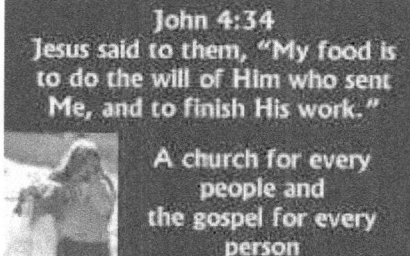
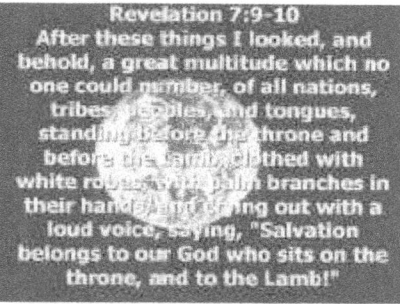
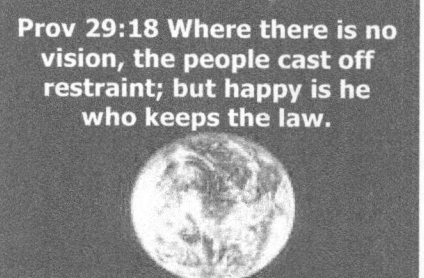
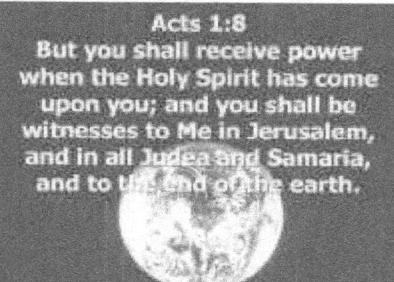

INTRODUCTION This message is not an attempt to help you focus on your own problems, struggles, finances, etc. If a house is on fire with children inside, why should it concern me if my nails are not filed and polished, my clothes are not designer or a house only has 1½ bathrooms! The multitude of Revelation 7:9-10 is the goal and the focus. We must keep our eyes on the true gold, the true purpose for living.

Facts About the World

a. 1.6 billion never heard the gospel, 27% of the world's population[1]

b. 16,000 languages have no scripture, no native pastor or church to attend

c. 95% of the world's pastors live in 5% of the world population. Only 9% of the world speaks English and 96% of the churches income is spent among the 9%. There are 37,000 Protestant missionaries from the US and Canada and all over the world. They come from 620 Protestant agencies working in 182 countries.

d. There are 2 billion Christians (33% of the world's population), 1.2 billion Muslims, 811 million Hindus and 360 million Buddhists.[2]

Facts About the USA

a. 35 million Hispanics in the US, 20 million of those are under 30 years of age[3]

b. 10 million Asians[4]

Empowering Your Preaching

c. Ethnic groups are now 36% of the total population.[5]
- The second largest Cuban city in the world is Miami.
- The second largest Mexican city in the world is Los Angeles
- The second largest Filipino city in the world is Los Angeles.
- The second largest Korean city in the world is Los Angeles.
- The second largest Samoan city in the world is Los Angeles. In fact, there are more Samoans living in the US than there are living in Samoa.
- The second largest Polish city is Chicago

d. Citizens of 200 countries attend our universities

e. International students are now 450,000. 45 past foreign presidents attended US universities.

f. 6-7 million Muslims in the US and about 1,200 mosques. Experts say Islam could become the second-largest religion in the nation within a matter of decades.[6] There are 10,000 Muslims and 6 mosques in Portland!

g. 2.4 million Hindus in the US

h. For the first time in history, representatives from every nation on earth live in one place—America.

God is a World Person
Oswald J. Smith: His church in Toronto, Canada has contributed 23 million do missions since 1928. He says, "The supreme task of the church is the evangelization of the world. When God loved, He loved a world. When He gave His Son, He gave His Son for a world. When Jesus Christ died, He died for a world. God's vision is a world vision. That is the vision He wants us to have."
John 3:16; John 1:29; II Corinthians 5:19; Matthew 24:14
- World Christian Attitude: Links my small circle of activity to the global community. It reminds me that my Christian faith rises above cultures; it knows neither national boundaries nor ethnic limitations.

I. **OUR VISION**

    A. Our CBC Vision Statement (Eph 3:20; Gen 49:22)
- **EXALTING THE LORD** by dynamic, Holy Spirit inspired worship, praise and prayer. Giving our time, talents and gifts as an offering to the Lord.
- **EQUIPPING THE CHURCH** to fulfill her destiny through godly vision, biblical teaching and pastoral ministries, bringing believers to maturity in Christ and effective ministry, resulting in a restored triumphant church.
- **EXTENDING THE KINGDOM** of God through the church, to our city, our nation and the world through aggressive evangelism, training leaders, planting churches and sending missionaries and mission teams.

Empowering Your Preaching

B. Our vision is to be:

1. **An international, multi-cultural church.** We have always desired to reach the nations of the world, but we are learning that the nations are literally here at our door. We want to build a bridge of love and trust to the people groups of our city. The central part of our strategy is to target different areas and people, reach out and build relationships, gather them in ethnic fellowships, and welcome them into the family as one church. *"... no longer foreigners and aliens, but fellow citizens with God's people and members of God's household"*

2. **A world vision church.** *"Therefore go and make disciples of all nations…baptizing…teaching them to obey everything I have commanded…"* There are 239 nations and 350 large world-cities that need apostolic churches. We need a world faith for a world vision! We by ourselves can't do this, but we can partner with the Body of Christ, mark our cities and do our share.

3. **A bridge building church.** There is no doubt that you have seen a bridge and it is equally likely that you have traveled over one. In fact, most of us have constructed a bridge. Who hasn't laid a plank or log down over a small stream to cross without getting their feet wet? A bridge provides passage over some type of obstacle: a river, a valley, a road or a set of railroad tracks. The type of bridge used depends on various features of the obstacle. The main feature that controls the type of bridge is the size of the obstacle.

4. **A Great Commission church**; this vision is vital to any healthy local church. From the outset it provides a sense of purpose and direction for the people of God. The Holy Spirit desires that we learn to think globally and eternally. (Acts 1:8)

II. **TOUCHING THE WORLD NECESSITATES BEING TOUCHED FIRST (Isaiah 6:6-7)**

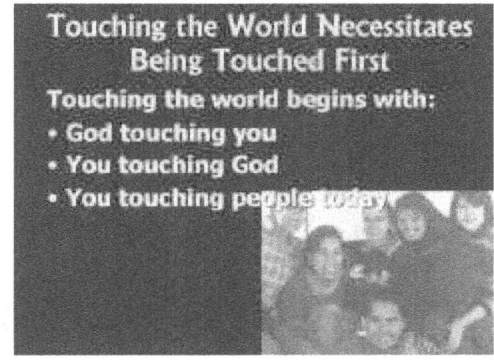

A. Touching the world begins by God touching you.

Empowering Your Preaching

      1.   CBC Member Profile: "The goal of our ministry to every member is to help them become a person who is born again, water baptized and filled with the Spirit, who is faithful to the corporate church gathering, cell ministry and School of Equipping; joyfully gives their tithes and offerings, enjoys prayer and worship, has a heart for winning our city to Christ and a vision for world missions, upholds family values and loves God with all their heart, soul, mind and strength.

      2.   God desires to touch your heart.

  B.   Touching the world begins by you touching God
      1.   When you reach out to God and touch His fire, His burden for the lost, you will change.
      2.   When you touch God, you touch His love, passion and compassion.

  C.   Touching the world begins by you touching people today
      1.   The Coles touched Laotians here in Portland first and then the nations of the world.
      2.   The way to become a world-touching person is to begin with first steps: people and giving.

III. OUR RESPONSE

- C.T. Studd, famous Cambridge rugby player and missionary to China: "If Christ be Lord and he died for me, then no sacrifice can be to great for me to make for Him."
- Winston Churchill: "Give us the tools and we'll finish the job."

  A.   Touching Our World: A Personal Response

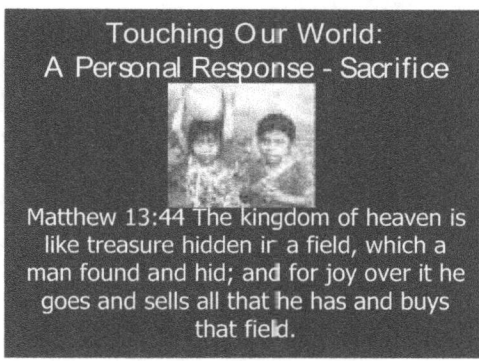

      1.   Sacrifice: <u>Buy the Field</u> (Mt 13:44)
Field = The harvest of souls the world over
          a.   Treasure = The work of God and of the Holy Spirit within the field. The treasure is the people.
          b.   Commitment = Sell all he has; total commitment to that vision. Possess the field; possess the treasure. Must make it a priority commitment.
          c.   Simplicity has to do with reorganizing your priorities of time and money to make room for missions.

      2.   <u>Equal Reward</u> (I Samuel 30:24)

Empowering Your Preaching

B. Touching Our World: A Corporate Response (Lk 12:48; Ps 2:8)

1. A commitment to becoming a Great Commission church

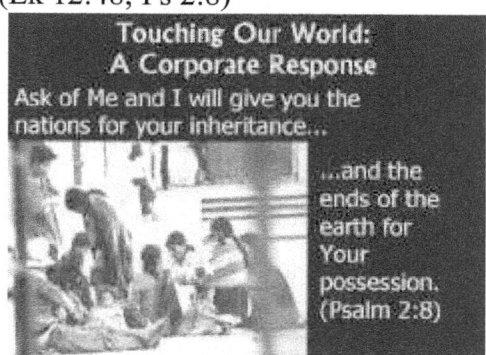

2. A commitment to developing Holy Spirit-inspired strategies to reach our world

3. A commitment to intercessory prayer for "all nations" of the world

4. A commitment to sacrificial giving of our best leaders to missions work

5. A commitment to sacrificial giving of our money, now, today for missions (Mt 6:19-21)

6. Planned Giving
   - Missions giving is one way to reach out. If you can't go, send someone else. We must get the job done.
   - John Wesley: Through sacrifice he helped others. He lived a simple life but gave over $500,000 to missions. "Gladly would I again make the floor my bed, a box my chair, a box my table, rather than that men should perish for want of the knowledge of the Savior."

---

[1] Status of Global Mission, 2001, in Context of 20th and 21st Centuries, January 2001.
[2] Status of Global Mission, 2001, in Context of 20th and 21st Centuries, January 2001.
[3] U.S. Census Bureau, Census 2000, unpublished tables (Table 9; March 20, 2001).
[4] U.S. Census Bureau, Census 2000, unpublished tables (Table 1; April 2, 2001).
[5] Gerry Johnson. *Preparing the Congregation for Ethnic Ministry* (paper presented in Portland, Oregon, November 18, 1998).
[6] Gustav Niebuhr. *US Muslim Population Flourishing* Oregonian ()

Empowering Your Preaching

Net Power and Principle
Building, Repairing and Extending Relationships

Weaving Through Building Relationships

Pastor Frank Damazio

Using the image of a net, Jesus teaches spiritual principles that the disciples would use in extending the Kingdom of God. Jesus teaches with wisdom from the natural world of fish, nets, boats, water. Every person can understand his language and it is very difficult to miss his point. To accomplish kingdom exploits, you need to have a net, a well-made net that will not break under pressure. To launch out into the deep, you need a boat and understanding of how to let go our your net. If your net is to last, you must be wise to stop and wash the net from all pollution and impurities collected by the net while it is in use. If the net breaks, you must stop and mend the net before it is totally destroyed and becomes unraveled. You must learn how to preserve your net.

Luke 5:1-10
1. The <u>making</u> of a net – *their nets* – weaving through building relationships
2. The <u>washing</u> of a net – *were washing their nets* – washing through Holy Spirit cleansing and purity
3. The <u>casting</u> of a net – *launch out into the deep and let down your nets for a catch* – willing to get involved with people
4. The <u>mending</u> of a net – *and their net was breaking* – watchful for relational rippers

Net Principles
- The <u>making</u> of a net – weaving through building relationships
- The <u>washing</u> of a net – washing through Holy Spirit cleansing and purity
- The <u>casting</u> of a net – willing to get involved with people
- The <u>mending</u> of a net – watchful for relational rippers

Luke 5:1-10 So it was, as the multitude pressed about Him to hear the word of God, that He stood by the Lake of Gennesaret, and saw two boats standing by the lake; but the fishermen had gone from them and were washing their nets.

Then He got into one of the boats, which was Simon's, and asked him to put out a little from the land. And He sat down and taught the multitudes from the boat. When He had stopped speaking, He said to Simon, "Launch out into the deep and let down your nets for a catch."

But Simon answered and said to Him, "Master, we have toiled all night and caught nothing; nevertheless at Your word I will let down the net." And when they had done this, they caught a great number of fish, and their net was breaking. So they signaled to their partners in the other boat to come and help them.

And they came and filled both the boats, so that they began to sink. When Simon Peter saw it, he fell down at Jesus' knees, saying, "Depart from me, for I am a sinful man, O Lord!" For he and all who were with him were astonished at the catch of fish which they had taken. And Jesus said to Simon, "Do not be afraid. From now on you will catch men."

Empowering Your Preaching

I. **UNDERSTANDING THE WORD NET**

A. Net = a fabric made by interlocking thread by knotting and twisting them at the points where they cross each other. The strength of the net depends on the number of twists or knots made. The net must be pulled and stretched into place.

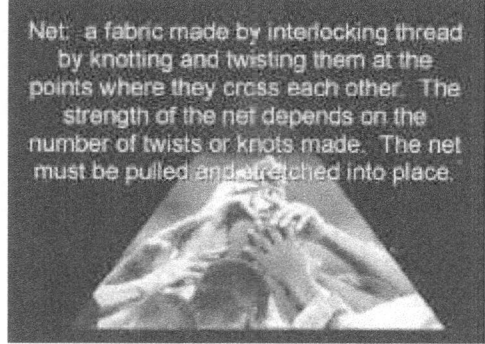

B. The Net: Scriptures and Key Phrases
1. Knit together (Eph 4:16; Col 2:2)
2. Joined together (I Cor 1:10; Eph 2:21)
3. Built together (Eph 2:22)
4. Many members (I Cor 12:26)
5. One body (I Cor 12:12-14)
6. Joint supplies (Eph 4:16)

C. The Networking Benefits
1. Safety
2. Fellowship
3. Encouragement
4. Increased faith
5. New friends
6. Other viewpoints
7. Teamwork
8. Joy
9. Unity
10. Added resources
11. Accountability
12. Immediate pastoral care
13. Worship intimately with other believers
14. Interconnectedness
15. Blessed
16. Loved

II. **THE WEAVING PROCESS – BUILDING AND SUSTAINING RELATIONSHIPS**
Why are relationships so complex if God meant them to be so important? We all need to and want to make relationships healthier and happier.
- Isolation
- Loneliness
- Disillusionment
- Fear/hurts
- Disappointments
- "There is no substitute for the comfort supplied by the utterly-taken-for-granted relationships."
- "Intimate attachments to others are the hub around which a person's life revolves."

Empowering Your Preaching

A. Weaving Begins by Embracing Biblical Concepts of Relationships

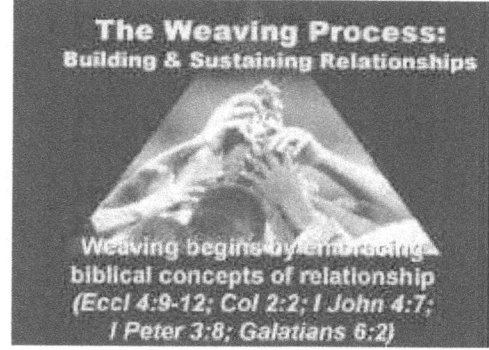

Who Packed Your Parachute: Charles Plumb a US Naval Academy graduate, was a jet pilot in Vietnam. After 75 combat missions, his plane was destroyed by a surface-to-air missile. Plumb ejected and parachuted into enemy hands. He was captured and spent six years in a communist Vietnamese prison. He survived the ordeal and now lecturers on lessons learned from that experience. On day when Plumb and his wife were sitting in a restaurant, a man at another table came up and said, "You're Plumb! You flew jet fighters in Vietnam form the aircraft carrier Kitty Hawk. You were shot down!"

"How in the world did you know that?" asked Plumb. "I packed your parachute," the man replied. Plumb gasped in surprise and gratitude. The man pumped his hand and said, "I guess it worked." Plumb assured him it did. "If your chute hadn't worked, I wouldn't be here today." Plumb couldn't sleep that night, thinking about that man. He says, "I keep wondering what he might have looked like in a Navy uniform: a white hat, bib in the back and bell bottom trousers. I wonder how many times I might have seen him and not even said, 'Good morning, how are you?' or anything because you see, I was a fighter pilot and he was just a sailor!" Plumb thought of the many hours the sailor had spent on a long wooden table in the bowels of the ship, carefully weaving the shrouds and folding the silks of each chute, holding in his hands each time the face of someone he didn't know.

Now Plumb asks, "Who's packing your parachute? Everyone has someone who provides what they need to make it through the day." Plumb also points out that he needed many kinds of parachutes when his plane was shot down over enemy territory. He needed his physical parachute, his mental parachute, his emotional parachute and his spiritual parachute. He called on all these supports before reaching safety. His experience reminds us all to prepare ourselves to weather whatever storms lie ahead. As you go through this week, this month, this year, this life...recognize people who pack your parachute.

1. Ecclesiastes 4:9-12

2. Colossians 2:2

3. I John 4:7

4. I Peter 3:8

5. Galatians 6:2

   The Scottish Farmer: His name was Fleming and he was a poor Scottish farmer. One day, while eking out his living for his family, he heard a cry for help coming from a nearby bog. He dropped his tools and ran to help. There, mired to his waist in black muck, was a terrified boy screaming and

Empowering Your Preaching

struggling to free himself. Farmer Fleming saved the lad from what could have been a slow and terrifying death.

The next day, a fancy carriage pulled up to the Scotsman's sparse surroundings. An elegantly dressed nobleman stepped out and introduced himself as the father of the boy Farmer Fleming had saved. "I want to repay you. You saved my son's life" said the nobleman. "No, I can't accept payment for what I did," the Scottish farmer replied, waving off the offer. At that moment, the farmer's own son came to the door of the family hovel. "Is that your son?" asked the nobleman. "Yes," the farmer proudly replied. "I'll make you a deal. Let me take him and give him a good education. If the lad is anything like his father, he'll grow to a man you can be proud of."

And that he did. In time, Farmer Fleming's son graduated from St. Mary's Medical School in London and went on to become known throughout the world as the noted Sir Alexander Fleming, the discoverer of penicillin. Years afterward the nobleman's son was stricken with pneumonia. What saved him? Penicillin. The name of the nobleman? Lord Randolph Churchill. His son? Sir Winston Churchill.

6. Acts 2:42-46

7. I Corinthians 12:25-26

8. Romans 15:1

9. I Peter 4:9

10. Mark 6:30-31

B. Weaving Begins by Embracing the Biblical Concept of the Church as Family

1. Ephesians 1:5

2. I Peter 2:17

3. Matthew 12:50

4. I John 3:1

5. Ephesians 3:14-15

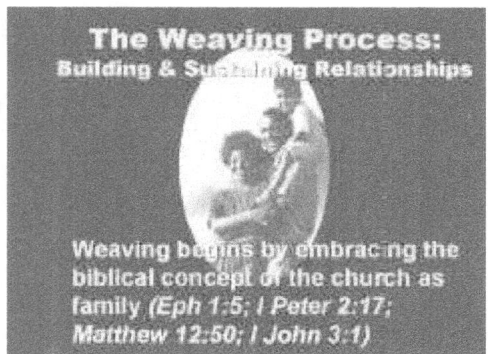

C. Weaving Begins by Facing Common Obstacles Hindering Relationships

    1. Unhealthy Individualism
- "Individualism lies at the very core of American culture. We believe in the dignity, indeed even the sacredness of the individual. Anything that would violate our right to think for ourselves, judge for ourselves, make our own decisions, live our lives as we see fit is not only morally wrong it is sacrilegious. As much as we want community, we shy away whenever it infringes on our autonomy!'" (Habits of the Heart)

    2. Fear of intimate relationship
- Fear of rejection, fear of embarrassment, not knowing how to be intimate

    3. Exhausting busyness
- People are working longer hours, both spouses
- School activities, community activities, church activities
- The pace of society is increasing

    4. Stressful and fractured lifestyles

    5. Laziness: don't want to work at it

www.ingramcontent.com/pod-product-compliance
Lightning Source LLC
Chambersburg PA
CBHW080335170426
43194CB00014B/2575